When the going gets tough – are you tough enough?

An exploration of independent social work

in recessionary times

Helen Ogilvy, Anne Sambidge and Gail C. Tucker

VENTURE PRESS

BASW Website: http://www.basw.co.uk

Published by
British Association of Social Workers
16 Kent Street
Birmingham
B5 6RD

British Library Cataloguing-in-Publication Data
A catalogue record for this book is available from the British Library

ISBN: 978-1-86178-085-0

Printed by:
Hobbs the Printers Ltd
Brunel Road
Totton
SO40 3WX

Printed in Great Britain

Contents

Foreword

When I patent my big idea and take it boldly out to the market and the public I will have this book by my side.

Many of us have our pipedreams but for the growing number of social workers who choose independent practice as the best way to use their skills in what is the best work in the world this is the key text.

Everyone who seeks and enjoys independence will benefit from the clear practical wisdom set out in these pages about how to manage your business well. However every policy maker and every commissioner should also take note of the commitment to the highest standards of ethical and effective practice which is set out herein.

If anything this book is at risk of selling itself short. In its relentless but necessary focus on what is real and up to date in England it is in danger of overlooking the rest of the world.

My recent visit to the World Conference on Social Work in Hong Kong demonstrated for me that this is an international profession with greater global respect than is usually apparent here. However most inspiring of all was the insight that many rapidly developing countries see social work as central to the development of their whole society.

Long before the living standards of Asian and South American countries eclipse our own it's clear that our social work needs to embrace the spirit of innovation and enterprise – allied to social work principle – that burns so brightly in these pages.

Now, about that big idea … oh yes and the next book…

Hilton Dawson

Chief Executive

BASW

Acknowledgements

We must start by saying a very big thank you to everyone who helped to bring this book to publication. From each of the contributors who gave their time so selflessly to the people who did all the technical stuff, for whom it has been a very hectic schedule, the countless individuals who just enabled us to make things happen and to Hilton Dawson, for writing the foreword – thank you all. We couldn't have done it without you.

Helen Ogilvy, Anne Sambidge and Gail C. Tucker

Notes on authors, co-editors and contributors

Authors and co-editors

Helen Ogilvy has been actively involved in the health and social sectors since graduating from St Andrews University with an Honours degree in Psychology in 1980. She is a qualified social worker (University of Wales 1985) and has worked within both the statutory and the voluntary sectors. She has been an independent consultant and trainer since 1994, specialising in community care issues.

Anne Sambidge established a private practice as an independent social worker in 1994 in order to continue to work directly at an advanced level with people who use services – at that time the only available alternative career progression was into management. Her broad portfolio of work plus her length and breadth of experience have resulted in commissions from a wide variety of agencies across the whole spectrum of work relating to children and families.

Gail Tucker qualified as a social worker in 1975 and after a career in local authority social work became head of the Member Services division of the British Association of Social Workers (BASW) in the early 1990s before establishing her social work consultancy in 1994. She has a particular interest in ethics in social care practice and much of her work now is with social care providers, reviewing services, advising and training on compliance issues. In addition, Gail acts in complex individual cases concerning safeguarding and mental capacity issues.

Contributors

Russell Hearth has been heavily involved in meeting insurance requirements for social workers for many years. He is responsible for running the Public Liability Scheme for BASW's independent members.
He has worked in the insurance industry for over ten years dealing with clients and insurers and he has worked for and dealt with many of the market leaders. He is currently working for OIM Underwriting Limited, which is part of Arthur J. Gallagher (UK) Limited.

Vic Knope is Divisional Director of Gallagher London who provide the BASW professional indemnity packages and he has been personally associated with the development of products for independent social workers for the past decade.

Colin Luger is an independent social worker and systemic family therapist working as an expert in courts in England and Wales with cases of parental denial where young children have been seriously injured. He also works half a day a week in a CAMHS team and is a visiting lecturer at the University of Bristol, and the University of the West of England.

Richard McNeilly is a partner at the Birmingham office of Dains LLP, a regional accountancy partnership, where he became Head of Business Development in 2006. He has extensive experience in the banking and financial services sector and specialises in working with small and medium sized enterprises and owner managed businesses.

Eddie O'Hara is a registered independent social worker and qualified primary teacher with over 25 years' ongoing experience of working directly with children and families, including adoption, fostering, investigating, reviewing, safeguarding and professional supervision. Eddie is also an independent social work trainer specialising in safeguarding issues, serious case reviews and effective social work practice and an associate trainer with BAAF, OUK, UNICEF and Warwick University. Over the last ten years Eddie has worked independently throughout the UK and Ireland as well as the USA and Turkey.

Dinah Tuck is a partner at Bates Wells and Braithwaite London LLP where she has been a solicitor for many years, covering both public and regulatory law and health and social care matters. As well as a broad diet of public law and litigation, she has specialised in advising and representing clients in matters such as professional regulation and registrations, safeguarding, inquiries and inquests. She has also, over a period of 20 years, worked on a variety of issues with BASW and has been a regular attendee at the annual BASW Independent Social Work Conference where she has run workshops on the legal topics covered in this book.

Introduction

It was one of those days when you hear yourself saying 'yes' to some proposal and later wonder whose bright idea that was!

Following the success of the first book in this series – *Independent Social Work – A Risky Business* (Tucker et al.; 2006) we had not thought of writing another one but on meeting in London in early March 2010, it had to be admitted that the world of independent social work had changed very markedly.

Independent social work is now a very much acknowledged part of the social work 'landscape'. The British Association of Social Workers (BASW), the organisation that sponsored the formalisation of a network for independents nearly a decade ago and had enabled several conferences and other events, as well as the book, had seen a very sharp increase in the number of members belonging to its BASW Independents network and using new services geared to them.

Such was the success of this that the organisation has since brought BASW Independents into its mainstream activity with allocated staff time and significant development work in progress.

And then there is the recession. This word was resisted by policy makers and politicians for quite a long time but it is pretty clear now, as was apparent from the budget of the first coalition government for a century, that tough times are definitely here to stay for the foreseeable future. So what impact is the recession likely to be having on those who are already working as independents and is there any prospect of anyone starting such a business in this climate? Are the skills required the same as those described in *A Risky Business* or have they changed?

This book examines these issues and looks at the particular challenges, both professional and business, of these difficult times. You will find that several central themes run through the book, to which we return several times. You may gain some comfort from knowing that you are not alone. You may glean some new ideas about how to survive and how to take advantage of new opportunities that inevitably arise from the rapidly changing social work agenda and likely cutbacks in public services. It may help you to decide whether to start a new business at this time, or to conclude that this is not for you. Well not now!

The book carries a 'health warning' because it has been written in such changing times. As we go to press, each new day brings announcements of cuts and changes to existing and proposed services, legislation and the landscape of organisations with which we are familiar. It represents a snapshot of this historic moment in time and will undoubtedly be overtaken by events as the years roll on.

Maybe we'll deal with that in the next book …

Chapter 1

Getting started and keeping going

As in the first book in this series, we make no pretence that this chapter contains all the answers; indeed, it may only provoke more questions! It introduces some of the central themes of this book, to which we return in later chapters.

Many would regard starting a new independent social work business in a recession as very ill advised. Indeed, it may not be an ideal environment but there are still many opportunities. Experienced practitioners who find themselves redundant when their former employer is forced to make budget cutbacks or someone wishing to change course during a period of austerity in public services may seriously consider it.

For those trying to steer their existing business through turbulent and changing times, the ever-present anxiety of whether the phone will ring and whether there is sufficient income to pay the outgoings each month remains the overriding concern.

Ethical framework

Whether starting out on a new venture or taking stock of an existing one, it is important to remain grounded in the ethical framework within which professional social work exists. This is formally expressed in the Code of Ethics of BASW, which we believe to be the only such code to specifically address the role of independent social workers. The Codes of Practice of the various social work regulators have general application and have guidance for independents.

In venturing into the world of business it is important to make sure that your customers know of the value base upon which your conduct will be based. Make copies of the Codes so that they are available to those who are unfamiliar with them and use the opportunity to spread the word.

Expertise

What experience tells us is that the knowledge, skills and strategic thinking required to set up a new business are the same as those required to steer an established business through the difficulties thrown up by recessionary times.

Having a clear view of what expertise you possess and how flexibly this can be applied is critical. This is no time for false modesty, nor for bravado. A candid assessment of all your professional strengths and weaknesses is essential. Talk to a trusted 'mentor' to get an objective opinion. Assess your training needs and seek courses or other opportunities to address any obvious shortfall.

A rational assessment of your personal and family circumstances is also essential. Are you free to take a big risk with your career at this point? It is going to be an economically difficult environment for the coming few years and running a business through that is not for the timid. You are probably going to have to work at least as hard as you ever have done and quite possibly a lot harder in order to stay afloat. The financial rewards will be variable and the risks considerable. If this is a time when you need to seek the greater security of employment for all or part of your working time, this is a good time to take that decision. Many independents have some employed work, some independent work and may also receive work through employment agencies.

Don't be beguiled into thinking that your social work knowledge is the only knowledge you will need in order to run a social work business.

Whether you operate as a self-employed individual, through a partnership or as limited company, you are subject to a wide range of legal constraints, which are managed by the employer. The chapter on legal issues addresses some of the key areas but you may need to join a business organisation such as the Federation of Small Businesses (FSB) and attend specific training courses to make sure that you have a full understanding of what you need to address. You certainly need to join as many networks as possible, which will keep you informed of new developments, usually through email bulletins. Recession tends to result in more change, rather than less!

Finding the market

Researching the constantly changing market remains vital. Even established businesses need to be aware that the organisations and individuals who contract the services of independent social workers directly are themselves undergoing tremendous upheaval. Here in the middle of 2010 we await pronouncements on the future of many publicly funded services. There is a mood of dismal expectancy in the air surrounding health and social care services, with new ventures being kept on 'hold'.

In such a climate it is likely to be the most knowledgeable, wider-experienced social workers who are likely to find independent work. The ability to be very flexible and respond to change is going to be key to business survival. Organisations will be looking for specialist expertise to steer them through difficult times and, in particular, to meet the plethora of changes taking place in the statute and policy arena. Making sure that you remain abreast of those changes may be the way to create and maintain business opportunities.

Because of all the change, organisations will also be running on reduced levels of staffing. When staff are 'let go' from public, private or third sector organisations, they are commonly the most experienced. These people can often move into another job more easily or retire but they frequently take with them a significant part of the organisation's intellectual resources and this is usually only truly recognised once they are gone. This leaves a needy organisation, which may be a business opportunity for the independent social worker. Compliance with all legislation is still required, complaints will still need to be investigated, reviews held, court work to be completed to deadlines and so on.

Consider whether you are offering your service across the appropriate geographical area and service community. Changing the parameters by working further afield or extending into a different service user group can have a very significant impact on the uptake of your service but take care not to overstretch yourself or to work too far outside your experience.

Manage the money

Tough times are a good time to evaluate very carefully the actual costs of running your business to establish what fee levels you need to generate in order to make ends meet but set them at levels that are likely to be competitive. You may have a range of rates according to different types of work, which require different skills or attract different levels of risk. You may find that some old rates are no longer covering your costs. Be rigorous in your analysis because doing work which makes a loss can really only be justified if it is seen as a 'loss leader', which brings with it other, higher-value, work. Consider your risk profile and pay good attention to Chapter 4 on insurance for social work businesses to see how to manage the risk.

Cash flow management is of paramount importance in a small business, which may operate on small capital assets. Review your terms of business and your invoicing practice to ensure that if customers are late in paying, you have a consistent strategy for dealing with this plus the resources to carry you through. Otherwise you may need formal overdraft facilities. These were very scarce for a while but banks are now responding better to existing customers who need this facility although you can expect to have to produce evidence of your business plan and to explain your debt handling procedures.

In tough times it is tempting to cut back on expenditure that looks to be peripheral to the day-to-day running of the business but planning for the future must be part of the analysis. Purchasing newer and more efficient equipment or making use of tax breaks, for example, can release valuable time, which is your most expensive asset. Review your travel strategy. Is your vehicle fuel efficient (which also saves on insurance and road tax) and is it suitable for the travel that you actually do? Consider whether you are getting the best rates for rail travel and try booking earlier for planned trips. Last, but never least, don't forget that you are responsible for your own future – pension planning is not a peripheral but a big issue for all of us. Even if you have pension rights elsewhere you should continue to contribute whatever amount the business can afford in order to support your eventual exit plan. This is where your accountant can be so helpful. If you haven't got one, attend to this matter immediately!

Contract terms

This is an area that we are not accustomed to in those settings where we have generally worked as employed social workers prior to setting up our own businesses as independents. In the public sector the separation is structural and those who deliver services do not either commission them or take the money. As an independent social worker, you must do all three with equal efficiency. Many independents have found themselves in difficulty part way into a piece of work where lack of clarity at the outset has led to genuine misunderstandings – or given a loophole for the less scrupulous customer.

Always get a written agreement before commencing a piece of work no matter how well you know the customer. A simple exchange of letters can be sufficient but make sure that you have their commitment to the work and the payment *before* you start.

You need to continually review the business paperwork to ensure that it is working well for both you and your current customers. This may change over time as you move into new areas of the market. Is the contract format clear and unambiguous? Do the invoices meet the accountancy requirements of the business and enable you to keep an eye on the cash flow? Are the terms for payment clearly expressed and have you got consistent protocols for debt chasing? Are the terms suiting you or the customer? Make sure that you are in control of the contract and the terms for payment. You do not have to slavishly accept those that are imposed by a customer.

Legal issues

If you are intending to trade as a 'social worker' by name, you will be required to be registered with the appropriate UK regulator, usually in the country where your business is based. Do remember that the title of 'social worker' is protected under the Care Standards Act 2000. The benefits and risks associated with this status are explored later in this book but it is worth giving consideration to whether being registered is the appropriate and necessary course for you. Some independent social workers do not actually perform social work tasks in the course of their independent activity but act as representatives or consultants in the wider world of social care and beyond. In some such cases there may not be a requirement to register and if in doubt you should take advice from the regulator's advice line.

Equipment

In the early days of independent social work we found ourselves operating in fairly unsophisticated environments. It was usually safest to take your own equipment and manage the whole event. Nowadays, with technological advances pretty well implemented in all venues, you may not need to purchase your own hardware but just provide the content by email or memory stick. However, costs of essentials such as laptops and data projectors have reduced considerably so it will be a matter for you to judge. Make sure that you have the conversation at the point where work is commissioned and write it into the contract letter, to avoid embarrassing misunderstandings on the day!

Be prepared

Just as in the rest of your social work career, the unexpected is the norm. Make sure that you remain alert and constantly evaluate what you are doing. Invite written feedback wherever this is practical. It can be of enormous assistance in planning new services and good feedback is good for the spirits.

Don't expect that things will always go well but plan to minimise difficulties when they do occur. Remember, your reputation is only as good as your last piece of successful work.

Chapter 2

Legal issues explored

Introduction

All social workers have a lot of law to contend with in their daily social work practice, understanding the laws that govern what they do, such as the statutory provisions of the Children Act 1989 or the Mental Capacity Act 2005, or the law dealing with questions of confidentiality.

As an independent social worker running your own business, there are further legal requirements that you have to comply with. Some will be relevant to all small businesses, not just social work. In this chapter we look at some of the legal requirements that may be particularly relevant, including various registrations, which you may need to ensure that you have in place.

Care council registration

If you are to call yourself a social worker you will know that you need to be registered with the General Social Care Council in England (or other Care Council elsewhere in the UK), pay the annual registration fee, renew every three years and comply with the Codes of Practice and other registration requirements. For more information look at the following websites:

- General Social Care Council www.gscc.org.uk
- Scottish Social Services Council www.sssc.uk.com
- Care Council for Wales www.ccwales.org.uk
- Northern Ireland Social Care Council www.niscc.info

Vetting and barring scheme registration

You may also need to be registered with the Independent Safeguarding Authority (ISA) under the Vetting and Barring Scheme (VBS) – the new regime in England, Wales and Northern Ireland that aims to prevent unsuitable people from working with children and vulnerable adults. A separate but aligned scheme is also being set up in Scotland.

Note: The provisions outlined below concerning registration under the VBS reflect the position **before** the coalition government announced on 15 June 2010 that commencement of registration (which was to have begun on a voluntary basis in some cases from 26 July 2010) was to be halted pending a review of the new regime. You will therefore need to keep in touch with developments, to check if and when the following provisions will still apply. You can do this by checking with the ISA at www.isa-gov.org.uk where you can also register for updates.

There are a number of exceptions but, broadly speaking, you will need to register if you engage in regulated activity with children or vulnerable adults on a frequent or intensive basis, and if you do so with the permission of a Regulated Activity Provider (RAP).

Do you engage in regulated activity?

Regulated activity is broad in scope, as is the definition of vulnerable adult, so you should refer to the Scheme Guidance (available at www. isa-gov.org.uk) to check if what you do is covered. In summary, the most common types of regulated activity that you might engage in are as follows:

- First, if you carry out any of the following activities with children or vulnerable adults frequently or intensively or overnight:
  - teaching, training or instruction;

- care or supervision;
- advice or guidance for children (if it relates to their physical, emotional or educational wellbeing) or for vulnerable adults;
- treatment or therapy.

Bearing in mind that a vulnerable adult is someone 18 years or over who:

- is in residential accommodation (for example a care home or a residential special school);
- lives in sheltered housing;
- receives domiciliary care in their own home;
- receives any form of healthcare;
- is in lawful custody (for example a prison or remand centre, young offender institution, secure training or attendance centre, or an immigration removal centre);
- is under a supervision order (in contact with the probation service);
- receives welfare services providing support, assistance or advice to develop their capacity to live independently in accommodation, or sustain their capacity to do so;
- receives any service or participates in any activity provided specifically for people due to their age or any form of disability;
- is an expectant or nursing mother in residential care;
- receives Direct Payments in lieu of social care services; or
- requires assistance in the conduct of his own affairs (e.g. Lasting or Enduring Power of Attorney).

- Or second if you do any sort of work in and for the purposes of any of the following types of establishment, frequently or intensively, and that work gives you the opportunity to have contact with children or vulnerable adults:

- schools or pupil referral units;
- nurseries or other childcare premises;
- children's homes, hospitals or centres;
- children's detention centres;
- adult care homes.

What does frequent or intensive mean?

According to the Scheme Guidance, it is for you to decide at the end of the day whether you carry out an activity frequently enough for it to require registration. The guiding principle should be whether the activity allows a relationship of trust to develop, but usually frequently means once a week or more (except in health and personal care services where it means once a month or more). If your work involves you visiting different establishments, you only do this frequently, according to the Guidance, if you visit the same establishment at least once a week. Intensively means on four or more days out of any 30-day period. If you are unsure about any of this, you should refer to Annex B of the Scheme Guidance.

Do you need to register?

If you engage in regulated activity on a frequent or intensive basis, you are quite likely to need to be registered. There are, however, some exceptions (which are set out in the Scheme Guidance). One important exception that may apply to you is if you are self-employed as an individual and you only ever work with service users who engage you directly themselves, or through a friend or family member. This includes where you are engaged by someone who receives Direct Payments (even though they are vulnerable adults for the purposes of the VBS).

If, however, you are ever engaged by a third party to carry out a regulated activity (for example if you are contracted by a local authority), and you are subject to their management or control, then they would be your RAP and you would have to register. If you engage in regulated activity (frequently or intensively) with the permission of a RAP, you must register.

Even if you are not required to register, it may still be sensible to do so. You may find that commissioners expect it and service users would prefer it. It will also gives you peace of mind – engaging in regulated activity while not on the ISA register is, if registration is a requirement, a criminal offence for which you could be fined up to £5,000. It won't be a defence to say you did not know that you had to be registered, or that you just overlooked it, so it is much better to err on the safe side.

When to register?

Note: The following provisions about when to register are now 'on hold' pending the coalition government's review of the scheme.

You will need to check with the ISA, but if in due course you are still required to register, then once the new commencement dates are known, the position (based on the existing legislation and guidance) is likely to be as follows.

Anyone who starts work carrying out a regulated activity (frequently or intensively and engaged by a RAP) after the new commencement date will have to register before they start that work. The same applies to those already working but who start a new regulated activity role with a new RAP after that date, which would affect independent social workers commencing a new contract after that date.

For those who work regularly but not continuously for a particular RAP, the Scheme Guidance suggests that you wouldn't have been treated as a new starter when you engaged on your next piece of work for that RAP after the first registration phase (which was due to start in November 2010) began. The Guidance says (page 38) that if you are carrying out periodic activity with the same RAP and, while you may not have had contact with the vulnerable groups for up to a year, you expect to resume the activity and have written confirmation of this, you may not apply to be ISA registered straight away. You will need to check the details of this once the new implementation arrangements are published. It is very important not to get it wrong.

How to register?

Registration is straightforward (unless it 1 urns out that there is a question mark over your suitability to be registered, in which case the ISA will consider under a separate process whether to bar or register you). The application to register is made to the Criminal Records Bureau (CRB) through a registered or umbrella body, and there is a fee (currently £64). You have to apply for registration to work with either children or adults or both. When you are registered, you receive a registration number, and then you are able to engage in regulated activity. You do not need to renew your application – it is a one-off application and once you are registered, that's it (unless you are at a later stage barred and removed from the register).

CRB disclosures

You may also need an enhanced CRB disclosure depending on the type of work that you do, although at the time of writing the government is also consulting on the ongoing requirements for CRB disclosures for those who are ISA registered.

Other VBS provisions

There are many other provisions in the VBS that you should know about, including the duties on RAPs to check an individual's ISA registration. This is on hold at the time of writing. There are, however, some other aspects of the VBS that still apply pending the review of the scheme. The ISA will continue to administer the lists of those barred from working with children and/or vulnerable adults, and it is still an offence for a barred individual to engage in a regulated activity (and for an employer to knowingly take them on). There are also still new duties on employers to refer information to the ISA if there are concerns that an individual poses a risk of harm to children or vulnerable adults. You can find further information about these and other aspects in the Scheme Guidance.

Data protection

If you are what is known as a Data Controller under the Data Protection Act 1998 (DPA), then you also need to register with the Information Commissioner and be aware of a number of other important data protection obligations that apply to you.

Who is a data controller?

You are a Data Controller if, as an individual or organisation, you (on your own or jointly or in common with others) decide how and why personal data about other people is, or is to be, processed.

What is personal data?

This is basically any information relating to a living individual who can be identified from that information on its own or combined with other information that is held and the information is more than just a passing reference to the person. This includes facts, expressions of opinions and indications of intentions about an individual. Information that is held manually (that is, not on computer or other electronic form) is not personal data if it is not held in an organised filing system – but don't let this encourage you to run a completely disorganised paper-based office! Best practice in any event is to treat paper records as personal data for the purposes of the DPA, especially when the information is confidential.

Information that relates to an individual's political opinions, racial or ethnic origins, mental or physical health, sexual life, religious persuasion, trade union affiliation or criminal record is known as sensitive personal data.

The person who the personal data relates to is known as the data subject.

What does 'processing' mean?

Processing covers virtually anything that you do with the personal data, not just using or disclosing it. It includes obtaining, recording and organising data, as well as even just holding or deleting it.

Are you a Data Controller?

If you are self-employed or running your own business and you are, one way or another, dealing with personal data about other people, then you are very likely to be a Data Controller. It is possible, however, that you might not be if you only work for a local authority or other public body carrying out statutory social work functions, or if you only physically process data on someone else's behalf and under their direction

Obligations on a Data Controller

In summary, these are:

- to notify the Information Commissioner;
- to comply with the eight data protection principles;
- to comply with certain rights of the data subject.

Notification

Notification is relatively quick and simple. You can get the notification form and guidance notes from the Information Commissioner's Office (ICO) by downloading them (www.ico.gov.uk) or by telephoning the Information Commissioner's notification helpline on 01625 545740. There is a fee (currently £35) for notification (assuming your organisation does not turn over more than £25.9 million each year and employ more than 250 staff!).

Once you have notified, your details as a Data Controller are published on the ICO's public register, and you have to renew the registration each year, paying an annual fee (also currently £35).

Some Data Controllers are exempt from the requirement to notify, for example if you only process manual personal data. But even if you do not have to notify, you can still choose to do so. It is certainly not worth taking any risk on this as failure to notify when you are required to do so is a criminal offence for which you can be fined up to £5,000. The fact that you are registered with the ICO might also help to convey that you have a professional and business-like approach to your work.

The eight data protection principles

In summary, the principles that must be complied with by Data Controllers are that personal data must be:

- processed fairly and lawfully;
- obtained and processed only for one or more stated and lawful purpose(s);
- adequate, relevant and not excessive in relation to the purposes for which it is processed;
- accurate and, where necessary, kept up to date;
- kept for no longer than is necessary for the purposes for which it is processed;
- processed in accordance with the rights of data subjects;
- kept secure;
- not transferred outside the European Economic Area without adequate protection and safeguards.

If you fail to comply with these principles, the Information Commissioner could take enforcement action against you, and/or the data subject could sue you for compensation.

There is plenty of information about all of this on the ICO's website (which you should read to get the full picture), but in practice, these principles mean that at the very least you need to think about the following:

- Ensure that so far as is practicable, the people whose personal data you have, know that you have it and what you are going to do with it. For example, when you see a client, make sure they realise if you are taking notes and tell them what you are going to be doing with the information that you gather.
- Don't do anything unlawful with the personal data – for example don't use or disclose it in a way that would breach a duty of confidentiality.
- Make sure that for every act of processing, either the data subject has consented (which must be explicit, that is, express an informed consent where you are processing sensitive personal data) or at least one of a number of other conditions is met. The other conditions depend on whether or not the personal data is sensitive.

  For non-sensitive personal data, the other conditions include where the processing is:
  - necessary to ensure you comply with a legal obligation on you (other than a contractual obligation);
  - necessary to protect the vital (life and death) interests of the data subject;
  - necessary for the administration of justice or for the exercise of a statutory, governmental or other public function in the public interest. (This would include where you are required by law, for example by a court order, to disclose information.)
  - necessary for your legitimate interests (or those of the person to whom you disclose the data) so long as the data subject is not prejudiced in an unwarranted or unreasonable manner.

  For sensitive personal data, the conditions are more onerous. The most straightforward is that you have the data subject's explicit consent. If you don't then the other conditions that you can rely on include where the processing is:

- necessary to protect the vital interests of the individual (where their consent cannot be given or reasonably obtained), or the vital interests of another person (where the individual's consent has been unreasonably withheld);
- necessary in relation to legal proceedings, for obtaining legal advice, or otherwise for establishing, exercising or defending legal rights;
- necessary for administering justice, or for exercising statutory or governmental functions;
- in the substantive public interest, for the provision of confidential counselling, advice, support or any other service and is carried out without the data subject's express consent because it is necessary where such consent cannot be given;
- in the substantive public interest, for the prevention or detection of an unlawful act and it must necessarily be done without the explicit consent of the data subject so as not to prejudice those purposes.

- Only use the data for the purposes of your work.
- Only hold and use as much personal data as you really need for your legitimate purposes.
- Don't keep personal data for any longer than you need to.
- Keep personal data securely. Use passwords on email attachments, and use encryption where you have personal data on laptops and other portable devices, which can more easily be lost or stolen.
- Destroy and delete information securely – don't do what one local authority was recently reported to have done, leaving copies of social work files in a filing cabinet that was then sold second-hand!

Rights of the data subject – subject access

Individuals have a number of rights in relation to data held about them. The one that crops up most often is the right of access to personal data (usually referred to as 'subject access'). You need to be aware of the rules around this, not least because if you fail to comply with a proper request you may be subject to enforcement action.

What is the right?

Broadly speaking, if a data subject makes a request in writing, provides sufficient proof of identity and pays a fee (which you set up to a maximum of £10), they are entitled within 40 days to be told what personal data you hold about them, what you are using it for and to whom it is or may be disclosed. The data subject is also entitled to receive copies of their personal data. This applies to all the personal data that you hold in relation to them on computer or manually as part of an organised filing system.

Exemptions

There are some occasions when a Data Controller does not have to comply with a subject access request, for example if it would involve disclosing personal information relating to another person (unless the other person has consented or it is reasonable in all the circumstances to disclose the information about them without their consent).

When you are weighing up whether it would be reasonable to disclose information relating to another person without their consent, you would have to take into account any duty of confidentiality you owe to the other person, whether you have tried to obtain their consent, whether they are capable of consenting and whether they have expressly refused it. If you do disclose someone else's information without their consent, it would be sensible to keep a note of the steps you went through and why you thought it was reasonable to disclose in the circumstances.

If you cannot obtain the other person's consent and you are not satisfied that it is reasonable in all the circumstances to disclose the information about them without their consent, you may still be able to provide information to the data subject without disclosing the information about the other person by simply deleting or blanking out their name and all other identifying particulars. If you can do this, then you should.

You would also be exempt from the obligation to comply with a subject access request where disclosure would prejudice the prevention or detection of crime or the apprehension or prosecution of offenders. You should also always make sure not to act in contempt of court where for example there are restrictions on disclosing documents in court proceedings.

There are also various specific exemptions in relation to local authority social work records, which do not have to be disclosed if for example disclosure would prejudice the carrying out of social work because it would be likely to cause serious harm to the physical or mental health or condition of the data subject or someone else. Also, if such information is requested by someone other than the data subject (for example someone with parental responsibility for a child), the information should not be disclosed if the data subject gave it not expecting it to be given to the person making the request, or has expressly indicated that it should not be given to that person. Also, a person is not entitled to information about them which is contained in adoption and parental order records and reports, where disclosure is already prohibited or restricted by other laws.

Requests by children and third parties
Children under the age of 16 can make subject access requests if they have a general understanding of what it means to exercise that right. If you receive a request from a child, there is guidance on the ICO's website to help you decide if you should comply with the request. The suggestion

is that in many cases children over the age of 12 would be likely to have sufficient understanding.

In other cases where a request is made via a third party you will need to be satisfied that the third party is entitled to act on behalf of the individual. This might be where the individual has given their written permission or where there is a relevant power of attorney.

Defamation

Defamation is an area where you are more vulnerable than your employed colleagues. If an employee makes a defamatory statement in the course of their work, action is much more likely to be taken against their employer than against them personally. You don't have the same comfort behind you as an independent social worker and so it is worth taking on board a few key points.

In simple terms, action may be taken against you if you communicate to a third party a defamatory statement about someone else.

What makes a statement defamatory?

A statement is defamatory if it would tend to make ordinary and reasonable people think less of the person about whom it is made, in other words, a statement that damages their reputation. Sometimes this is obvious, for example a statement that someone has committed a criminal offence or if you make a serious attack on their professional ability or judgement. But other times it is less clear cut.

A defamatory statement is libel if in writing (including email and text messaging), or slander if spoken – both come under the global term of 'defamation'.

Sometimes you may defame someone without meaning to, or knowing that you have. It is not just literally what you say that counts, but also what your words would be understood to mean. Also it is not just how they would be understood by an ordinary bystander, but also how they would be interpreted by people who knew the particular context and surrounding facts and circumstances. You should therefore take care to be clear in what you say or write, so that you don't inadvertently make a statement that carries a defamatory meaning that you did not intend (and you can't defend).

Who it refers to

You should also try to avoid inadvertently referring to someone you did not intend to refer to. Sometimes a defamatory statement can be understood as referring to someone you have not even named or singled out. Again, it all depends on who it would be understood as referring to, not who you meant. Incidentally, you can defame companies and charities as well as individuals. However, you cannot currently be sued for defamation by a local authority or government department.

Publishing a defamatory statement

A crucial element in an action for defamation is that you must have communicated or 'published' the defamatory statement to a third party. You can also be held liable where the person you made the statement to, passes it on to someone else, even if you did not ask or intend them to. It just depends on whether you should reasonably have anticipated that the spread of your defamatory material was a natural consequence flowing from you making the statement in the first place. If you only intend a document to be read by certain people, mark it personal and confidential, and send it securely, remembering in particular that emails and faxes can easily be picked up and read by other people. Remember too that more than one person can be liable in respect of a defamatory statement – anyone who passes it on or is responsible for its publication (or re-publication). It is no excuse therefore to say that you were not the original author of the statement and you were only passing it on.

Defences

Your work may inevitably involve you in making defamatory statements about other people quite frequently. But all is not lost, as there are of course a number of defences. For a start, no action will succeed in respect of a true statement of fact (though bear in mind that the onus would be on you to prove it was true, and not just what you literally said but also the 'sting' of it).

Another defence that might be relevant is qualified privilege – where the law recognises that there are occasions when you should be able to speak freely without fear of action being taken against you. An example of this is where you are under a duty (which might be social or moral, not just a legal duty) to make a statement to someone with an equally legitimate interest in receiving it. That might be where you report an allegation to the correct authority, or you prepare a report and send it to whoever commissioned it. If, therefore, you limit what you say to what you genuinely need to say, and to people who genuinely need to receive it, then you are quite likely to be protected by qualified privilege. That is, provided you do not act with malice – there is no protection if you make a statement that you know is untrue, or if you are reckless about whether or not it is true, or if you had an improper motive in making the statement.

Reports prepared, and evidence given in court proceedings, should also be protected to the extent that the contents are relevant and are used only for the purposes of the proceedings.

Finally, in all the areas of law mentioned in this chapter, there is much more to them than we can tell you here. You should be aware that this is a general overview, whereas your particular circumstances may need particular consideration, and possibly independent legal advice. But it should help you to reduce your risks if you carry an awareness of these issues.

Chapter 3

Accountancy for social work businesses

Choosing an accountant

On the face of it, choosing an accountant is a simple process. Across the UK, there are thousands of well-qualified practising accountants able to support a small business. In addition, the internet now provides access to the whole market and even broker services offering low-cost alternatives. However, when choosing an accountant, careful consideration should be given to the type of support and advice your business requires. The nature of support will vary at every stage of your business – through start-up, while growing, upon exit and beyond.

Ask yourself the question: do I want an accountant to work with me in order to ensure that my business is compliant, tax efficient, profitable and successful or should I choose the lowest-cost option? A successful working relationship between advisor and business can last for a lifetime and it makes sense therefore to conduct some form of 'beauty parade' before choosing an accountant.

A proactive accountant will generally provide a free one-hour consultation and in order to get the most from your meeting, consider writing a checklist. The checklist could include areas such as:

- What services are provided as part of the fixed fee arrangement?
- Who is my main contact and how can I gain access to them?
- Are there specialist advisors available to advise on matters outside of the normal compliance cycle (for example, complex tax, mergers and acquisitions, business growth advice)?

- How often can I expect to meet with the accountant and what are the related costs?
- Can the accountant provide specific references in the areas I feel are most important, such as tax or planning for growth?
- Does the accountant recommend an accounting package given what they know about my business? If so, is training available and what are the related costs?
- What is the most appropriate business structure for my business and why?
- Does the business need to register for VAT? If so, what information is required?

At the initial meeting, a proactive advisor will generally discuss with you the most appropriate structure for the business, considering all options available, such as sole trader, partnership, limited liability partnership and private limited company. Equally, you can expect some basic tax advice, which will shape your decision as to which business structure to adopt. Finally, a proactive advisor will spend time in understanding you and your business, along with your future objectives, as well as telling you about their own range of services. If an accountant spends little time at the outset getting to know you and your business, you are probably in the wrong place – quality advice comes with sound knowledge of you and your business.

Record keeping

Depending on the business structure, a number of statutory returns are required. As a minimum you can expect to complete a self-assessment tax return to Her Majesty's Revenue and Customs (HMRC). A limited company is also obliged to file annual returns and annual accounts. As the business grows and takes on more staff and pays additional benefits such as company cars or private healthcare, other issues come into play – often involving HMRC. Speak to your accountant about what statutory returns are required and what are the important milestones to reach before becoming subject to additional submissions.

A well-managed business will maintain close control of cash and profitability. Every business is different and there is no 'one size fits all' accounting package in the marketplace. Depending on the size of your business your accountant will provide advice as to whether your business should seek additional input from a bookkeeper, and whether the business requires a full accounting package or indeed a financial controller/financial director. Some businesses are run very effectively using simple tools such as spreadsheets and straightforward bank reconciliations in order to maintain records. Work in conjunction with your accountant in order to generate an appropriate level of control for the business while maintaining costs at a sensible level.

However simple your processes are, please keep in mind the fact that accountants charge for time and good-quality orderly records should enable your business to minimise the cost of professional advice and ensure that time spent with your accountant is adding value to your business rather than costing you money. In the early days, there is real merit in your accountant reviewing your systems in order to prevent misunderstandings. An hour spent in reviewing systems can prevent days and weeks of time correcting errors or attempting to reconcile poor-quality data.

Tax and tax Planning

Taxation is an incredibly complicated area and it is advisable to obtain advice from your accountant *before* making key decisions such as business structure, remuneration and capital purchases. Tax legislation changes frequently and, as an example, in 2010 we have experienced two budgets and one pre-budget report, all of which will impact on small businesses in some way.

Tax planning should take account of the business and the key individuals within it. Good advice is not limited to ensuring that key staff are paid as tax efficiently as possible but rather, should include advice on remuneration, exit planning, capital purchases, inheritance tax planning, property matters, changing legislation ... the list is endless.

VAT is another complicated area, particularly where businesses provide a range of products and services. Good-quality advice from your accountant will enable you to ensure that you are aware of the need to register for VAT or otherwise and whether there are any cash flow benefits available in changing the basis for payment of VAT. It is vital to gain a thorough understanding of how VAT impacts on your business from the outset. Many business owners outsource completion and submission of regular returns to their accountant and so help is generally available should you require it.

Contingency planning

While not always written down, every successful business has a business plan. If experience teaches us anything, it is that however much you plan, things never quite work out as you expect them to do. As a result, it is vital that for business continuity the business has some form of contingency plan.

In these difficult economic times, a key consideration is cash 'headroom'. Headroom is normally measured by the amount of cash you have available before your business requires additional financial support, which could come in the form of third party funding or by cash introduction for example. There is no magic formula for calculating the correct level of headroom but some simple analysis will help. For example, it may be useful to consider the impact of your clients failing to pay for a few months, or replacement costs of a key employee in the event of long-term illness. Always ensure that the business has a reasonable cash buffer – the unexpected will probably happen.

Too many businesses fail because they are under-capitalised from the outset and can't cope with the unexpected, be it a delayed payment, a bad debt, a fire or long-term illness of a key employee. If your business does not have sufficient headroom to trade at the outset then consider seriously whether you should be going into business at all. Better still, raise sufficient funding in order to cope with the unexpected before it happens – very often funders are more likely to support the business that thinks about problems before they happen rather than the business that looks for help in the event of a crisis.

All of the issues raised above have implications far beyond the financing of a business. It is vital therefore to consider a disaster recovery plan – effectively, to plan for the unforeseen. Thinking through the process of what your business should do in a calm environment (as opposed to post disaster) has real merit but once again this should be completed at a level commensurate with the size and complexity of the business. Breaking down the business into key areas such as finance, human resources and operations will help formulate the plan. Ensure that key staff know about the plan and how to find it should they ever need to do so.

Pension planning

Good-quality businesses have a keen eye on succession and will generally work towards an exit plan. Well-run profitable businesses sell for substantial amounts of money and despite the economic downturn, we are seeing a return of good-quality mergers and acquisitions activity.

However, many business owners leave intellectual property and goodwill in the hands of too few people, which ultimately results in low business valuations. Unfortunately, many business owners conclude that the business is their pension fund, but often find that the capital sum they dream of is not forthcoming. Succession planning and exit planning are emotive issues for everyone involved in the process. Working alongside your accountant often helps the process to stay on track. Your accountant will not carry the same emotional baggage and will help to rationalise the plan to all stakeholders. Very often those businesses that have worked to a plan (for exit) and have groomed their business generate substantially higher valuations than those that don't.

We recognise that many independent social workers embark on this course later in life, after a successful social work career in an employed position. Planning for exit need not be left until the last few years. Many businesses take advantage of favourable tax breaks to make pension provision throughout the life of business. As with any investment there are pros and cons to consider and dialogue between your accountant and financial advisor is vital. Watch out for changing legislation with regard to pensions both in terms of both staff and individual contributions.

Chapter 4

Insurance for social work businesses

Introduction

When money is in short supply and you are looking for ways to trim your expenditure, the one area where you should not take risks is the area of insurance. Over and above legal requirements, this is an important means of managing foreseeable risks to your business. There will always be a plentiful supply of things that remain unforeseen but there are a number of risks that can be anticipated and having insurance in place will help in managing those risks.

When starting a business you may have to make adjustments to your existing insurances so we will look at those first.

Vehicle insurance

It is essential to make sure that your vehicle is insured for you to use in the course of your business. Many comprehensive policies cover the business use of the policy holder in person but you will need extended cover if you are likely to carry business equipment, which may include computers or projectors. If you carry official passengers, such as colleagues or people who commission or use services, your insurer needs to be aware of this. Failure to disclose all the facts to your insurer may result in you finding that you are not covered by the policy in the event of a claim. In the case of an accident this may lead to prosecution as well as the massive financial implications of uninsured losses.

Home and office insurance

If you have separate premises you will obviously need to hold separate buildings and contents insurance for them. Many people do not realise that even when you work from your own home you need to inform your household insurer and to ensure that your office contents are also insured. Some insurers do not offer such policies but many will just extend an existing policy for a small, additional premium. If you have professional visitors to your home you will also need to look at public liability, which we deal with below.

Health insurance

All small businesses where the expertise is centred in one person become very vulnerable if that person develops an illness or becomes incapacitated, particularly if this is a sudden event. The service that is offered may be disrupted or lost completely and, along with it, the income stream. There may be other costs if contracts involve penalty or performance clauses.

There are some policies that provide a wide range of health cover and which pay out if you become an inpatient or during certain courses of treatment that prevent you from working. A different form of insurance is 'critical illness' cover, which protects by paying an agreed sum on being diagnosed with one of the listed specific conditions set out in the policy. These policies are particularly important if you have family responsibilities that need to be maintained if a serious illness overtakes you.

All health insurance tends to be quite expensive and in most cases the costs rise over time because the risks gradually increase in line with the age of the policy holder. Some policies will have a cut-off at a certain age, which may be some time before your retirement.

Income protection insurance

It is still possible to insure against loss of income itself. This type of policy pays out if you can prove that your income is lost. These policies are less available than previously, before the present financial cutbacks, and again tend to be expensive to take out currently. One difficulty that some people have experienced is that in order to meet the very stringent wording of some policies it would be necessary to wind up the business! Take independent advice.

Employer's liability insurance

If you have set up a company and have employees you will be required to have this type of cover to protect your staff. This covers all risks in the course of a person's employment, including accident and injury. In many small businesses, individuals often take on more than one role and multi-task. There are many providers of such insurance but it is wise to find one that specialises in small professional businesses as they will understand your risks better than others that specialise in larger organisations.

Public liability insurance

In recent years the need for all social workers to carry insurance has increased many-fold. There are many reasons for this, some of which you may have seen reported in the recent press, but mainly because local authorities no longer offer protection to their social workers. Most local authorities used to cover the claims arising from their social workers but over the years this declined and now the responsibility falls directly on the social worker.

Particularly relevant when times are tough and the 'claims culture' is so exaggerated, it is essential that independent social workers carry relevant insurance to protect against any claims that could arise from day-to-day social work tasks and activities.

People are often confused about what each type of policy covers. Public Liability insurance is there to protect you against claims arising from third party property damage, bodily injury, mental injury and, in extreme cases, death. In simple terms, if you damage another person's property or someone is injured due to your negligence then a claim can be brought against you to recover the cost for the damage or pay compensation in the event of personal injury.

You are likely to be well aware of media advertisements by solicitors and specialist claims' handlers, along the lines of 'have you had a trip or fall that was not your fault?'. These are the most common forms of public liability insurance claims. You may wonder how this might affect you. In your role as a social worker, you are in constant contact with the general public and you have a responsibility towards them when they are in your care or you are entering their homes and other agencies' buildings while you are acting in a professional capacity. If a claim should be brought against you and the correct insurance is not in force, it could be very expensive for you. Not only would you have to pay any compensation and your defence costs but also the costs of the third party bringing the claim against you. However, if a public liability policy is in force at the time of the incident then the insurance would cover all of the costs involved in the action. However, please note that cover is not retrospective: it needs to have been in place before the claim is made.

A typical example of a public liability claim would be a visitor to your office who is injured when they slip on a spilt drink. Insurers will compensate the visitor for their injuries and associated expenses and will help to maintain the business relationship. This is absolutely invaluable in the event of an incident. Also, the expertise of the insurer in handling such matters can be very reassuring.

As you can see from this example, it is very easy for a claim to arise and sometimes an incident that appears to be quite minor at the time can rapidly escalate into something major. As an illustration, the cost of the settlement of the claim in the example given above was in the thousands of pounds – and that was just from a simple slip.

Public liability insurance can also extend to cover claims brought by governmental, administrative or regulatory bodies. Independent social workers are running businesses and so are subject to many forms of regulation under various statutes. The range of issues can be very wide ranging and however hard you try to be compliant, claims may arise. Just defending an action can be not only very expensive but also very time consuming for a small business. If any criminal action is brought against you during the period of insurance for any breach of statute or regulation, directly relating to any actual or potential claim, the insurers will pay the costs incurred to defend such an action against you or any of your employees.

Yet again, there is benefit in finding a specialist insurer that both knows the risks attached to your business and is used to dealing with small businesses. There are several providers but members of the British Association of Social Workers (BASW), have immediate access to quality insurance. OIM Underwriting Limited has produced a bespoke public liability policy purely for purchase by members of BASW. All you need to do to arrange this cover is to contact the membership team at BASW or, if you are already a BASW member, to ask for your name to be added to the scheme. The policy is offered by Hiscox Insurance Company Limited who are market leaders and were voted 'Insurer of the Year' in both 2008 and 2009. The company also has a highly regarded claims handling team along with teams of people to help you in the event of a claim arising. Wherever you purchase your insurance from you must be able to produce documentation for people who contract your services. Under the BASW scheme you will be provided with the necessary paperwork.

When making difficult decisions about how to manage the business through tough financial times you may wonder whether or not you can afford this cover. To put it bluntly, you cannot afford to be without it. Compared with the cost of an uninsured claim this is a very good buy in tough times. Many people assume that this type of insurance is very expensive for the level of cover you can obtain. However, if you take out the insurance through the BASW scheme mentioned above, you will be pleased to know that the cost is currently less than £200 per annum and in most cases can be paid on a monthly basis to help control your cash flow. The peace of mind that this relatively small annual outlay ensures is priceless.

As with all insurance policies there are, of course, certain areas that are not covered. However the insurers have tried to produce a policy that will protect you when you need protection.

The main exclusions of public liability insurance are claims that would be covered under other insurances such as professional indemnity (see below) or employer's liability insurance. Claims falling in these areas would be covered under the appropriate insurances. Other exclusions applying to all policies include terrorism, war, nuclear and asbestos related claims. It is important that you always read your policy documentation carefully to make sure that you are fully aware of all of the terms, conditions, limitations and exclusions. If you are not sure, take independent advice.

Professional indemnity insurance

As a class of insurance, professional indemnity is a relatively new one. Fifty years ago, it was fairly uncommon for people to try to recover money for any losses suffered from taking professional advice. If something went wrong, then the professional simply apologised and life moved on.

Things started changing in the 1960s. A landmark case called *Hedley Byrne v Heller* essentially established the now general view that, if you are a professional, it is reasonable to assume that people will follow your advice. Consequently, if things go wrong, any financial loss suffered could be brought to your door as the professional.

We have also seen a change in the public's attitude towards litigation. The advent of 'no win—no fee' litigation has removed the financial implications of embarking on litigation so there is absolutely no barrier to prevent people commencing a court action, no matter how far-fetched their case might be.

Of course, BASW recognised the need for professional indemnity insurance in the early 1990s and have had a scheme in place since then. If you are already a BASW member you have a standard level of cover within your membership package. Getting extended cover is both quick and easy to arrange at a slightly higher premium. Other organisations provide professional indemnity products but because BASW is recognised as being at the forefront of setting the standards for social work, underwriters reflect that in their prices. It is unlikely that an individual member could, on their own, get this level of coverage for the same sort of price.

In today's difficult economic , such protection is even more necessary. High-profile cases such as Victoria Climbié and Baby P have opened the public's eyes to the responsibilities and burdens borne by social workers.

Having frightened you by setting out the vulnerabilities, we now turn to how you can protect yourself and your business. Many of you will find that as you are being contracted as independent consultants, the option of whether or not you have cover and, if so, what level of cover you might buy, is not going to be a choice – it is often imposed on you by the terms of your contracts. Levels vary, but having good cover in place is a sign that you are a sound organisation to deal with.

We have already pointed out that there are some areas not covered by other policies. Professional indemnity insurance covers any successful claim made against you for errors or omissions in your professional practice. If you are considered to be at fault, Professional indemnity insurance will pay the claimant's loss together with any legal costs that they have sustained in putting forward their case.

As a registered social worker in the UK you may find yourself the subject of a complaint about your professional conduct to the regulator with whom you are registered. Such a case takes a long time to investigate and you may find that you are suspended from the Register during this period. This will prevent you from continuing to practise as a social worker until it is resolved and as a result your income may cease at exactly the same time that you find yourself facing considerable expense. A professional indemnity policy covers the legal costs that you might sustain in defending your position. Whether you are innocent or not, the legal fees can escalate at an astonishing rate. However, if something does go wrong and you have the appropriate policy in place, you can be reassured that your insurers can provide you with top-quality solicitors and, if necessary, barristers to defend your position.

There is no magic solution to protecting yourself against potential claims but here are a few hints on what you should do to limit the possibility of such a scenario:

- Be clear in your own mind the scope of the services you are providing and put them in writing to the people commissioning those services. All too often, professionals run into trouble when either they undertake things that they do not fully understand or, more significantly, the individuals or organisations contracting their services assume that the scope of duties which the independent social worker will be undertaking will be different from those that the professional is trained to cover.

- Do not ignore complaints. Occasionally, things do go wrong and if you are faced with a complaint then no matter how trivial, you should respond to it. Ignoring or failing to respond quickly to complaints is one way in which frustration and bitterness develops, which may contribute to the making of a claim.
- Keep clear records and have them available for future review. It will be much easier to protect your position if you have notes of any incidents or complaints made at the time when they occurred, rather than having to rely on your memory three or four years afterwards.
- Let your insurers know immediately about any problems that arise. Failure to report a loss at the right time could jeopardise your protection.

Conclusion

The very nature of social work means that it is highly likely that things will not always go right all of the time. The important thing is to be able to bounce back, learn from the experience, and move on. It is vital to remember that if you do not have insurance cover and a claim is brought against you then you could be in for a shock. The last thing you want to be thinking is 'if only I had taken the insurance'. In the words of Jean-Claude Favez, (1999), 'Of all the forms of wisdom hindsight is, by general consent, the least merciful, the most unforgiving'.

Of course, by protecting yourself with BASW's insurance you will be covered for a minimal cost with maximum coverage.

Chapter 5

Independent practice in children's services

It is not the strongest of the species that survives, nor the most intelligent that survives. It is the one that is the most adaptable to change. (Darwin, 1859)

Although Charles Darwin wasn't an independent social worker, one could easily argue that his insights into how species survive by adapting to their changing environments are applicable today for independent social workers in children's services. The reason why many very experienced independent practitioners are still working in this context is primarily due to the fact that in order to survive the ever-changing world of social work, you have to learn how to adapt your work to the changing environment around you, while still firmly holding onto your professional values and standards.

As reflected throughout this book, the political and economic landscape in which independent social workers find themselves simply reflects the broader dynamic micro-climate of social work in general. It is a landscape that on almost every level presents us with ongoing professional and business challenges.

These challenges include the planned capping of court fees for independent experts referred to elsewhere and the increasing growth of supermarket-style social work agencies, which in pursuit of market dominance are driving down national fee levels. Then there's the pressure on people who commission our services to save money at the expense of quality and experience and the competing professional targets being set by various bodies and others besides. It all adds to a growing perception that there is a significant mismatch between a government aspiration of 'improving and investing' in the standing and professionalism of experienced social work on the one hand, and the increasing level of savings being sought at every corner on the other.

Having said that, there is no doubt that the practice of independent social workers in children's services has come a long way during the past ten years and you will find independent practitioners working across the entire spectrum. However, the same two questions always seem to present themselves. First, how can an independent practitioner make a decent living working in children's services? Second, why after a year or so, do so many really good practitioners either return to work as paid employees for various social work organisations or simply leave the profession? Why can they not survive as independent social workers? In the great tradition of Darwin the explorer, this chapter sets out to examine these questions and to look at how independents are diversifying in order to survive the changing environment.

Making a living

To begin with, how can you make a living out of working as an independent social worker within children's services? To answer this question you have to honestly and simultaneously address a number of other questions:

- Why do you want to work independently?
- Are you self-motivated?
- Are you very good or even excellent at what you do? If not, why do you think anyone will pay you to provide a service for them?
- Are you reliable and organised?
- Are you professionally supported by your peers?
- Are you able to demonstrate leadership within your sphere of work?
- Are you registered to practise?
- Are you flexible enough to meet your clients' needs?

- Are you prepared to spend up to 20 to 30 per cent of your time effectively working for free as you run your business, seek out new clients and nurture existing clients?
- Are you clear about what your skills set is and who your customer base is likely to be? It may include local authorities, solicitors, voluntary agencies, schools and many others.
- Given that for most independent social workers, the vast majority if not all of their new work comes as a result of direct recommendations from other professionals, are you able to promote yourself as someone who is non-partisan and has a niche expertise?
- In a profession where staff turnover is endemic, are you able to offer a consistency of service that sets you apart from your peers? Contrary to the popular perception that independents have no commitment to children and families and simply come and go, many families benefit from having the consistent support of an independent practitioner long after other employed or agency staff have moved on.
- Are you able and willing to use your independence and freedom from organisational constraints to evidence a developing range of complimentary skills in working with children and families (safeguarding, preventative work, adoption, fostering, family placements and mental illness to name a few) or are you simply a 'one-trick pony'?
- Do you recognise and can you work with the incongruities that are involved when some commissioners undervalue (in monetary terms) direct work with children and families and yet seemingly overvalue non-direct work such as consultancy, training and non-direct reviewing?

It is highly likely that if a prospective independent has not asked themselves these fundamental questions or their answers to them are predominantly 'No' then the risk is high that they will soon be part of the growing number of former independent practitioners!

Survival of the fittest

Among those independents who continue to survive in the arena of children's services there do appear to be some common themes and attributes. To start off you need to have an inner resilience and ability to value your own work, particularly at those times when it might seem as though no one else does. Despite the recent hyperbole in the social care media about how important social work is, the reality is that for the most part, the social work profession generally commands very little respect or status from the public, other professionals and sadly sometimes even from within its own ranks.

Unlike professionals who work in health or education, most positive social work activity is not recognised, acknowledged or valued by anyone, other than perhaps the recipient of that activity. Therefore working for the most part with devalued and disempowered families on your own, and frequently in isolation from other professionals, without a traditional manager or supervisor there to reassure, encourage and praise you, means that you need to be able to both critically evaluate and also genuinely value the true worth of your own work. You also need to be able to accept that for the most part that has to be enough.

You also need to understand what it means to work independently, to be able to value and protect your professional independence of mind and soul and avoid becoming simply a hired hand ready to go along with something that you feel compromises either your professional standards or social work values.

Given the increasingly 'macho' management style that exists in many children's services, you need to be able to differentiate between a professional mindset and professional practice that promotes leadership skills and child-centred decision making, and unquestioningly promoting non-child-centred resource-led management.

You need to develop a sense of business awareness and be able to anticipate where demand for your services (skills set) will be in the next twelve to eighteen months. Given the unpredictable nature of service provision and its funding, you need to be able to predict and anticipate where the next cuts will fall and where opportunities might open up. Remember that many large independent providers in the children's sector employ people for the express purposes of trying to predict where and when the next opportunity will be and then planning for this accordingly. You need to be able to do that for yourself.

An ever-changing environment – or evolutionary forces?

On a general level, with the recent election of a coalition government whose number one priority is to reduce the national debt, we have already seen a realignment of social care within a new Department for Education, the scaling back of the Independent Safeguarding Authority, the planned end of Contact Point, and the abolition of the National Safeguarding Delivery Unit. Ironically, at the same time that we as a profession are facing huge cuts, the new coalition government has commissioned yet another review, this time by Professor Eileen Munro, to look into how those working with children and families can be more effective!

All of this would suggest that the recent political spotlight, which in the wake of several child death tragedies briefly shone on social work with the creation of the Social Work Task Force (and the subsequent creation of the Social Work Reform Board), is now clearly moving in another direction. The independent social worker has to be very fit indeed to keep up!

Nowhere is the government's lack of understanding or appreciation of just how much independent social workers contribute to our profession to be found, than by considering how the Legal Services Commission (LSC) is planning from October 2010 to cap fee rates at approximately

30 to 50 per cent lower than the current independent social worker professional rates and significantly lower than those charged by other related professionals.

Diversification

Working within this context of continual change and cuts in funding, independent practitioners have found over recent years that they have increasingly had to broaden out the type of social work they do, the arena's in which they work, the clients with whom they work and the skills set that they have. No longer is it possible or wise to rely on one or two sources of employment, or to offer only a select number of services.

A couple of examples of diversification from a very experienced independent practitioner are:

- Working in partnership with a Sure Start Centre and a health authority in providing safeguarding training and consultancy – what is striking about these arrangements is just how much added value an experienced independent practitioner can provide these organisations and professionals in terms of specialist safeguarding knowledge and advice;
- setting up another company with colleagues from related disciplines to provide independent specialist investigations into issues of professional conduct – this has enabled them to combine their collective professional skills and apply them to a variety of social care and non-social care settings in both the public and the private sectors.

In so far as becoming involved in new areas of work is concerned, like all new ventures it is not as easy as it sounds, so do be prepared for knock-backs and failures along the way. You also need to recognise that while you may have many transferable skills, frequently there will be occasions when this is not enough and that in order to progress you will need to set about adding to your skills set. Those independent social workers who lack such professional insight and fail to recognise their own professional limitations have frequently come to a sticky end.

If you are serious about pursuing a career as an independent social worker, then like any self-respecting and credible professional you also need to be involved in a variety of professional bodies and forums. This is not simply to keep your own skills and expertise up to date, but also to ensure that you have a voice in shaping your profession and the context in which you work.

With reference to the issue of the LSC plans to cap fee rates, many independent social workers have been actively involved through both BASW and the National Association of Guardians Ad Litem and Reporting Officers (NAGALRO) in helping to bring pressure to bear on both the LSC and the Ministry of Justice to ensure that the proposed caps are not introduced. This is not only so that children and families can continue to have access to high-quality and experienced independent social work assessment and opinion in court proceedings, but also to ensure that there is not a further exodus of practitioners willing and able to provide services in this context. Sadly, if the planned caps on fees are introduced, then with a profound sense of regret, many highly regarded practitioners have made it clear that they will no longer be in a position to afford to continue taking on publicly funded court cases. Given the wealth of experience of those individuals, diversifying into other niches will not be a problem for them. The problem will lie elsewhere.

Why do it?

So why, if it is so hard, do so many people prefer working independently? There are probably as many reasons as there are practitioners but here are some of the reasons we hear most often:

- You have the flexibility about what work to do, where to do it when to do it, and for whom to do it.

- You have the flexibility to work across the whole spectrum of children and families work and the additional insights that this experience brings.

- You have the opportunity to establish your professional credibility based on current, direct, frontline practice where on a daily basis you can draw on social work theory, develop and refine your professional skills and engage with the public. It means that you may meet with senior managers or government advisors in the morning to talk about policy, then a few hours later be working directly with the very families who experience the effects of these policies. It means that when people ask you if you are now a legal expert or social care management consultant, you can proudly and truthfully say 'No, I'm a social worker and it's the best job in the world'!

- Most importantly, you can still create opportunities to increase your social work skills working directly with the very children and families many of us first trained as a social worker to help. For many highly experienced social workers this remains the only real professional activity which feeds and sustains their 'social work soul'.

So what does this all mean for those who want to pursue a career working as an independent social worker in children's services at a time when the political climate surrounding our profession is so uncertain? It means that there are still great opportunities out there for creative practitioners, as long as they remember a few of the following points:

- Working in children's services, the independent social worker's sole focus is to promote the wellbeing and interests of children and families, not themselves. If you do this well, others will see it and reward you. If you simply focus on your own needs, others will see this too and your reputation and work will soon dry up.

- Recognise and then positively use the parallels of feeling 'out of control', which you may feel as an independent working alone, with how children and families feel when they are involved with social workers in statutory settings.
- Be supportive of your employed colleagues; remember they will generally be under different, and often much more uncontrollable pressures than you.
- Hold on to your professional values and use them to help you navigate what at times can be the stormy seas of working independently.
- The standard of work that you do today will directly affect the supply of work you have tomorrow. From a prospective client's perspective, you really are only as good as your last piece of work.
- To survive recessionary times in children's services you need to be ready to embrace change and be prepared to adapt to your new professional surroundings. If you ignore 'change' and are not prepared to at least try to adapt, then there is little doubt that like all extinct species, sooner, rather than later, you will be consigned to history. For those creationists among you, put another way, functional theory tells us: that which has no function simply ceases to exist!
- Even the most experienced and confident independent social workers have many moments of self-doubt as they take on new areas of work. The trick is to prepare as best you can for it, call on as much support and help as you can, 'feel the fear' and then simply get on with it!
- To get involved with other independent social workers and professional bodies to prevent you from becoming professionally isolated.
- To regularly remind yourself to appreciate just what a great job being an independent social worker is and how important your role is.

Finally, don't forget that just as Darwin is remembered long after his death for his contribution to our understanding about how species survive change and evolve, good independent social workers are frequently remembered by children and families long after they are no longer directly involved in their lives, simply because of the profound, positive and long-lasting impact that their previous professional involvement has had upon their lives. Seriously, who could ask for a better job?

Chapter 6

Working with adults

Many independents with extensive experience were initially trained generically and continue to work across sectors. The separation of public sector services into children/families and adult services is not necessarily replicated in private and voluntary sector services, thus these generic skills can be particularly helpful to many organisations. Families and individuals are often bemused by these artificial divides in legislation, entitlement and provision and they, too, can find this generic understanding particularly helpful. Given that under the Personalisation Agenda it is likely that adults will increasingly have the option of purchasing their own services, with the option of someone independent to manage that on their behalf or to guide them, then it is easy to see that these generic skills are likely to be advantageous, whether working with individuals or with organisations.

However, some people do elect to become more specialised, focusing their work on adults generally or with a much more specific focus such as mental health, head injury, older people and so on. Whether you opt for genericism or become specialised to a greater or lesser degree, one message is clear – in tough times the best strategy is to maximise what you have to offer and be prepared to diversify. However, we argue strongly that this should be neither diversification at any price nor diversification beyond the margins of your competence and confidence. No matter how tempting the prospect might be, it simply isn't worth the risk – for you or for other people. Maintaining your reputation for good practice and good outcomes continues to be the best form of advertising. It is important to safeguard that reputation at all times, but particularly when opportunities may be sparse.

Working with adults occurs in many settings and calls upon a variety of knowledge sets. In this chapter, we consider the range of opportunities in working with adults who use services and their carers, working with policy makers and working with service provider organisations.

Working with adults who use services and their carers

Carrying out an independent assessment of needs for an individual is perhaps the most obvious place to begin this section. This assessment may be commissioned by the person themselves to help them make appropriate plans for their own care, particularly if their financial resources are such that they would be paying the full cost for services if they were assessed and subsequently received services that are arranged by a local authority in England or Wales. On the other hand, it may be commissioned by a solicitor acting for the person in relation to a complaint about the accuracy of a local authority's assessment or the level or type of care that is being provided to meet the identified eligible needs. Alternatively, it may be commissioned by the court, as described in Chapter 7 on expert witness work.

Carers who are providing, or intend to provide, regular and substantial care to an adult or a disabled child also have the right to an assessment of their needs and in some circumstances this may be something that is commissioned from an independent social worker by a local authority or an organisation acting on their behalf. A solicitor acting for a carer may also ask for an independent view on the carer's needs and the way in which they are being met. In many parts of the country, the number of carers' assessments completed has been much lower than expected and the outcomes from them variable, despite the introduction of NI 135, a Performance Indicator within the Department of Health's current National Indicator Set relating to the number of carers receiving an assessment, information or services. As a result, the pressure is very much on to provide more of these assessments within a system that is struggling to deal with all the other demands placed upon it.

Whatever the source of the commission, and irrespective of whether it is for someone who uses services or their carer, carrying out an assessment independently bears the same requirements in terms of accountability and professionalism. It also creates opportunities to work in a way that is consistent with the origins of the very word 'assessment'. It is derived from the Latin verb 'assidere', which means 'to sit beside'. This verb is also the root of the word 'assizes', with all its connotations of judgement. Thus, assessment in its true sense is a process of sitting beside someone, helping to make judgements about their situation and helping to plan ways forward – which is somewhat removed from many people's experiences of assessments in practice. One of the commonly heard frustrations expressed by social workers in statutory settings is that, despite fine words from the Department of Health in paragraph 47 of the Practice Guidance to accompany the Carers and Disabled Children Act 2000 (DH, 2001) that 'Assessment should not be a bureaucratic process based on ticking boxes', for most practitioners that is exactly how it feels. Working independently gives you much more scope to break out of that mould and practise in a much more holistic way. The greater challenge is to demonstrate the value of such assessments in terms of good outcomes and to educate commissioners that time and money spent on good-quality assessments, particularly when money is tight, is a good investment and much better than picking up the pieces when things go wrong or complaints mount up.

As public services contract over the coming years due to financial pressures, it seems likely that the number of legal challenges to decisions about assessed levels of need will increase. It seems likely, therefore, that the number of independent assessments that will be needed will also increase. However, as discussed elsewhere in this book, the level of fees that this work is likely to generate seems likely to decrease, so independents may have to think carefully about whether to pursue this area of work, rewarding though it can be in other ways.

In addition to assessment and subsequent care planning, what is often invaluable to individuals is to have someone to help them understand the complex health and social care landscape and to assist them in finding their way through it and to understand their rights. Hearing such information from someone who is knowledgeable about, but independent of, the system can carry a value all of its own – but again it rather depends on whether people are willing and able to pay for this invaluable advice. Many independents offer such a service for a limited number of clients at a much reduced fee or 'pro bono' as a matter of principle.

Similarly, having the services of an independent advocate to enable a person to articulate their views can be extremely valuable, whether in the context of assessment, reviews or complaints. Increasingly, private individuals are willing to commission such a service at a modest cost in order to help them achieve what they want to achieve. In some instances, particularly in complex situations, voluntary organisations whose remit is to provide such advocacy will commission an independent social worker to advocate if the organisation itself does not have anyone with the necessary specialist knowledge. A recent example from practices concern a voluntary organisation whose remit is to support carers. The organisation had been approached by a carer whose daughter with learning disabilities had been made subject to an authorisation under the Deprivation of Liberty Safeguards 2009. The carer felt that their views had not been listened to properly and that they had been marginalised in the process, despite the duty placed on assessors to consult with carers. They wanted to complain about this but needed support to do so. Given the highly specialised nature of this legislation, it was not unreasonable that there was no one within the voluntary organisation with the relevant expertise and understanding but they did not want to let the carer down. In response, the organisation commissioned an independent social worker, who was also a qualified Best Interests Assessor for the purposes of the Deprivation of Liberty Safeguards, to act as advocate for the carer. As a result, it was possible to resolve the complaint at an early stage to the satisfaction of all parties and with the added benefit of a number of recommendations to improve local practice in this emerging area of work.

Investigation of complaints is another area where the skills and expertise of independent practitioners are extremely valuable. While complaints processes try to resolve matters informally at a local level, in some instances it is necessary, and indeed good practice, to commission someone independent to investigate the matter. As recessionary pressures bite and services retract, it seems likely that complaints will rise, thus skilled complaints investigators are likely to remain in demand. In recent months, the Local Government Ombudsman service has found it necessary to seek independent practitioners to act as field investigators on their behalf in relation to both children's and adult services – another new opportunity for those with the requisite skills.

In addition to assessment, advocacy and complaints work, another potential avenue to explore is providing training for the people who use services and their carers. As the Personalisation Agenda develops, with people with assessed care needs having the option of Individual Budgets to purchase their own services, it is likely that a whole range of opportunities will arise to provide training to help people understand how to use those budgets, what their rights are and, for some people, how to be an employer. In fact, many people who choose to administer their own budget may find themselves asking the same sorts of questions that independent social workers and consultants have to ask themselves when starting their businesses, so there may be some natural links to make there.

There are also many opportunities to develop training for carers, particularly in light of the objectives of the 2008 Carers' Strategy entitled

Carers at the Heart of 21ˢᵗ Century Families and Communities (DH, 2008) and the funding streams that have arisen from this. Part of the vision is that carers should be recognised as expert care partners and so should receive training to enable them to understand the health and social care landscape and to equip them with additional skills in their caring role. At the time of going to press, it was not clear what the coalition government's position will be in relation to both empowering carers and allocating ongoing funding to this developing area of work. There can be no doubt, however, that the need is there and independent social workers and consultants are ideally placed to help deliver what is needed.

Working with policy makers

One of the advantages that many independents can bring to a situation is their generic and longstanding knowledge of social work and social care combined with an understanding of how social work fits with other disciplines. The good independent has an ability to 'read across' and to make links that are not always obvious to people with less experience. Yet these links, if recognised and worked with, can make the difference between something working well in practice and being an unmitigated disaster. These skills are profoundly valuable at the point where policy is being developed and where it is being translated into action at the front line. As long as we have government, we will have policy. As long as we have policy, there will be a need for such skills. Whether there is a stomach for them or, indeed, a budget to commission them is another matter and beyond the scope of this chapter.

Many independent social workers regard themselves as having an obligation to contribute to government consultations, which is now made easier by them being conducted online. As an independent you can say what you really believe, which may not be possible for those who are employed in the sector.

Working with service provider organisations

One area of independent work mentioned at the beginning of this book concerns working in an advisory or consultative capacity to organisations that provide direct services to a service user group or groups.

Many private and third sector providers, whether large or small, find themselves struggling with a variety of regulatory frameworks that the social care sector is subject to. The past decade has seen enormous legislative and policy changes across the sector and many organisations have found that they do not have the specialised knowledge and do not have sufficient staff resources to meet the demands. Added to this has been the pace of change. With hitherto unknown very short consultation and implementation timetables, the demands have been very alarming for those directors or trustees charged with the governance of an organisation.

Working at that level, an independent social work consultant can provide both the expertise and the additional available resources to inform the organisation, devise implementation plans, offer training to key personnel and provide quality assurance monitoring of the outcomes. The stakes are high in some cases, for example registration of care providers or, as in the case of England at present, compulsory 're-registration' due to a change of statute. Failure to deliver is not an option so no matter what it takes, the deadlines have to be met.

Many small organisations that cannot afford to maintain their own full-time staff for such a purpose will often form a long-term relationship with an independent consultant and then call on them for a wide range of support services. It is valuable to them, and good business sense for you, that you have a range of skills on offer so that you can deliver a seamless service from initial advice through to implementation and evaluation at the other end of a project. Working in collaboration with other independents can be one way of offering a full range of services and providing extra personnel without having to employ staff yourself.

Sometimes these contracts come from unexpected beginnings. A project that starts off with the confident assertion that it will last 'for about three months' may turn into several years of a happy association. These contracts are very worthwhile for both parties but you must beware that no single customer dominates your work to the extent that the HMRC might consider you to be an employee of the customer, and tax you accordingly. Working through a limited company can make this much less likely but it is very important to keep a range of customers on the books during the course of a year, even if one of them is the main fee earner. Always check this with your accountant if you have any doubts.

Sometimes an organisation will use you to act as their 'horizon scanning' facility, providing regular updates often to a number of customers of upcoming changes, with impact assessments and well ahead of the time when action will be required. Keeping up to date yourself is, of course, absolutely essential but a judicious and consistent use of electronic alerts, which are freely available from all government departments, quangos, improvement agencies and regulators, as well as from specialist private advisory services to which you might subscribe, can put you in a strong position. The service you provide is invaluable to organisations where the frontline staff are fully occupied with the day-to-day management of services that comply with existing requirements. There is no room for error. If you get something wrong the organisation's compliance or legal status may be put at risk.

Other organisations that want to deliver quality services often like to operate their own arm's length quality assurance monitoring, in addition to whatever procedures they have in-house. An independent social worker is well placed to provide management inspections and specific audits for trustees, directors or managers along with implementation strategies for rectifying any shortfall. Not only does this mean that the organisation is likely to be in good shape when various regulatory visits are made but it is a good indicator to the regulators that the organisation has an open and transparent approach to its service delivery and can learn from its own experience.

One of the specialist areas that lends itself to these approaches is that of safeguarding. Often the first call will be about an incident that has shown up a problem. Take an instance where a resident in a care home has died and there is to be a coroner's inquest as well as a safeguarding review by the local Safeguarding Board. A consultant can carry out an independent audit for the provider, and assist them to make such representations as may be required in the court and the formal proceedings. It would be usual to identify, with the provider, what management actions may be required. These may involve interventions with staff under their disciplinary or capability procedures. New or amended policy and procedures may be required and staff training to embed these. Successfully navigating such incidents can cement a long-term relationship with an organisation, which will lead to further requests for involvement, hopefully at an earlier stage next time in order that preventative strategies can be implemented.

Legislative and policy changes have a habit of being very volatile ground. During the last five years in social care for children and adults, for example, five new pieces of direct legislation have been given Royal Assent. Some have not yet successfully been implemented in full and as this book is being written a new coalition government is busy revising the 'progress' of some of them.

Rights for people who lack mental capacity have undergone massive changes with the implementation of the Mental Capacity Act 2005. However, the actual impact 'on the ground' has been very patchy indeed. Many individuals are happily carrying on as before, blissfully unaware that they do not have rights to act for their relatives or service users in their care. The implementation of local authority resources has been similarly challenged, which has resulted in little awareness being raised in local communities. Now that the country is cash strapped by a recession and as enormous cuts to public funding have been announced and more are anticipated, it is unlikely that this picture will improve. In the meantime, organisations and individuals who run into difficulty need a source of knowledgeable advice and often actual direct assistance to find their way through the systems of the Office of the Public Guardian and the Court of Protection. These procedures can be tortuous and very costly. Often fees are not forthcoming for very long periods, where they are publicly funded. When undertaking such work, make sure that the cash-flow implications for the business are well assessed and that contingencies are earmarked.

Chapter 7

Expert witness work

We are in the midst of a government-driven review of public spending and we can be sure that some areas will fare better than others. The political expediency of being seen to protect frontline public services may not translate into practice so it is even more vital that the importance of the role of social work is brought to the public's attention at this time and that arguments are made in the relevant arenas to protect its integrity and demonstrate its intrinsic value, both in the statutory and in the independent sectors. This chapter examines the contribution that expert social work witnesses make and argues that we must take account of the financial context we are working in to ensure that best practice and best value are delivered.

What is expert witness work?

The very name 'expert witness' suggests that at some stage the practitioner will be asked to go to a court or a tribunal to give evidence and this is often the case. In family proceedings, courts value expert independent social work opinions on issues such as the risk to a child living with domestic violence or the risk from sexual or physical abuse, assessing a child's attachment to a parent, sibling relationship assessments, human rights-based assessments for parents facing deportation, and whether a child can be placed within their wider family following a kinship assessment.

In the arena of adult services, an expert witness may be called on to offer a clearly evidenced opinion to the Court of Protection as to what course of action might be in the best interests of an adult who lacks mental capacity. Another example would involve giving a view to a Mental Health Review Tribunal as to whether a patient subject to Section under the Mental Health Act 1983 (as amended by the Mental Health Act 2007) still meets the criteria for detention or whether a less restrictive option would be more proportionate and appropriate to their needs.

However, expert social workers also work in many other arenas. They may be instructed by a solicitor who is acting for a client making a complaint about the actions of a local authority. In such instances, the solicitor may ask for an expert opinion as to whether the assessment of the person's or their carer's needs took full account of all the available facts and whether the conclusions it reached and the actions it led to were reasonable and proportionate. The report may then be used to negotiate different outcomes for the client without recourse to a formal complaints process or may be submitted as part of a formal complaint, which has the potential to lead to the Ombudsman's door. Another example of expert opinion might be where a service provider is considering developing a new service and wants an independent, well-evidenced view as to whether what they are proposing is firmly aligned with legal requirements and best practice and if not then some clarity as to what changes might be needed.

How is it perceived?

For most people, the idea of a social worker being an expert is not something that comes easily to mind. Compared to the medical profession where historically there has been a recognised body of knowledge and skills that can be measured and taught, for example how to diagnose a disease and treat it, social work comes with a different legacy. We still debate what social work is, how it should be taught and how it should be governed. The public image of social work suffers from frequent adverse publicity and the media's perception that it is seen to operate for the benefit of the disadvantaged and inadequate in our society. In other words, social work may be necessary but it is a necessary evil that reminds people of what they would rather not know, that parents and carers can kill their child (whether in childhood or as an adult with disabilities), and that there are communities of people who are vulnerable due to their age, disability or mental ill-health and who need protection, support, and advocacy. There are no 'quick fixes' in social work, just an engagement with human beings faced with a need that may be practical, emotional and even life threatening. We are often experts in the unthinkable.

Social workers have developed a body of skills and knowledge that is highly sought after in certain situations, for example where a court is faced with the question of whether to pursue the reunification of a child with a family where the child has been previously non-accidentally injured. There will have been expert medical evidence presented in court and a Finding of Fact that the child has or has not been subjected to non-accidental injury and by whom. If the Court finds that the child was non-accidentally injured and then determines the most likely perpetrators, it is faced with a dilemma as it has a duty to consider the right of that child to a life within its birth family. This example highlights the nuanced reality that social workers operate in. The media presents issues as very contrasted – it's either this or that, a parent is either good or bad, a wonderful mother or an evil killer – when the reality is rather more complex and a much finer judgement is called for. In such uncertain territory, expertise is required to help the court make the right decision for the child but that expert opinion will rightly be examined in court by the legal advocates and subject to the court's ultimate decision.

An expert witness offers an outside, independent opinion irrespective of who is instructing and paying them and the ultimate legal duty is to the court, and through the court to the welfare of the child or the vulnerable adult.

How does an expert become an expert?

Experience is one component but time served does not necessarily equal confidence and competence. The expert has to demonstrate an awareness of the body of knowledge that underscores their particular area of practice. The expert will not be a lawyer but must understand the legal or other context they are working in and the procedures that pertain there. If working throughout the UK, the expert must be well versed in the different legal structures and requirements in each of the four countries and respectful of these differences. Experts can easily be seduced into overstepping the boundary of their expertise, which they do at their peril. An expert who has developed an area of practice may be interested in working in a related area but interest does not equal expertise and at the back of the expert's mind must always be the question: *'Can my opinion stand up under hostile cross-examination?'* It is all too easy in the witness box for an expert to be invited to comment on something that is outside their area of expertise in order to be helpful to the court, but then rightly be shot down for professional arrogance.

The acid test of an expert's expertise is whether it withstands the test of time. Word of mouth among potential commissioners will bring new work if past commissions have been responded to appropriately. Word spreads as quickly about an expert's incompetence as it does about an expert's valued opinions. Over the years, there have been expert witnesses across the professions who were less experienced and knowledgeable than the court expected them to be, or who have strayed outside their area of expertise and who have subsequently paid the price when revealed. Whatever else, expert witnesses must be aware of what they know, but as importantly they must be aware of what they do not know – better to be a competent expert about one small corner of the field than claim to be an expert about the whole field.

Arguably, expert witness work is by its very nature an example of independent social work at its most valuable as it calls for high levels of skills, knowledge, expertise and integrity. It calls for true independence of word and deed. Reports and court testimony are usually based on in-depth work with clients and other parties. Very often, cases are at the forefront of developments in law and practice and the expert independent social worker has a key opportunity to contribute a holistic social work view to these cases. In the court arena, the independent social worker is responsible first and foremost to the court but always mindful of the best interests of the child or adult whose future is being decided. Away from the courts, in complaints cases where the independent social worker is instructed by a solicitor or commissioned by an organisation, their central responsibility is to the person who uses services and to their Codes of Practice. In both settings, the independent expert is well placed to give an honest and well-evidenced opinion to help reach the right solution.

Some examples

A highly respected consultancy was asked to undertake a risk assessment in a matter before the High Court. The case involved twins, one of whom had sustained serious shaking injuries at three months old, including significant haemorrhaging both to the front and the back of the brain and bilateral retinal haemorrhages. Blood tests were carried out to check whether the child had any rare metabolic disorder but the results were all negative and the opinion of the medical experts was that the injuries were non-accidental.

The evidence strongly pointed to the father being responsible for the injuries but he denied responsibility and the Finding of Fact hearing was not scheduled to take place for several more months. The children were placed with maternal grandparents with the mother living there as well but under the constant supervision of the grandparents. The father remained living in the parental home with his contact also being supervised by the maternal grandparents. The High Court judge wanted matters to be progressed as soon as possible in the children's interests and agreed to an assessment prior to the Finding of Fact hearing. The consultancy's conclusions were that despite the very real concerns, rehabilitation could be considered providing an appropriate programme of work was undertaken with the parents and members of their support network. This involved the mother being the lead carer and the father not being left alone at all with the children but able still to play a significant role in the children's parenting by following family safety guidelines with the support of the 'helpful adults' around the family who were involved in the work. The consultancy's recommendation for rehabilitation was opposed by the local authority although the children's guardian and judge were in agreement. The parents and children were once again able to be a family rather than remain apart, with all the long-term emotional impact that would have entailed, let alone the financial cost to society. However, this was only possible with expert assessment and further work borne out of years of experience.

In a case involving adult services, another social work consultant was instructed by a solicitor to produce a report relating to the needs of a man with mental health needs and a complex physical health complaint. The independent consultant was asked to provide an opinion as to whether the local authority had adequately assessed his needs, in particular the interconnected nature of his physical and mental health needs and whether the level of services provided were proportionate to those needs. The report was also required to consider whether the local authority had adequately considered the person's request for Direct Payments, an issue that had been outstanding for a number of years. The report was produced on the basis of three detailed interviews with the man and detailed analysis of previous assessment and care planning documents. After extensive negotiations, including some timely intervention from the Ombudsman, the local authority accepted that the level of service that it had been providing was not proportionate to the needs and it was increased ten-fold. Arrangements were put in place for the man to receive Direct Payments, allowing him a much greater degree of control over his care and lifestyle and the local authority made substantial back-payments. While the improved level of service and back-payments were important, the really important point from the man's point of view was that he was finally listened to and that resulted in change.

Immune from tough times?

Given this immensely valuable role, one might expect expert witness work to be immune from the effects of these recessionary times. In practice, this is not the case – independent social workers providing expert testimony find themselves in particularly challenging financial times and indeed many have already made the decision to focus their practice elsewhere.

In order to understand the nature of this challenge, we need to pose a very basic but inescapable question: what should an expert witness charge for their services? Being independent means having to pay for two very different aspects required to ably carry out that function. First, there is the hardware – the office as a place to work and maybe carry out interviews, the car, the computers and office equipment, a mobile phone and stationery. Second, there is the 'software', which demands the expenditure of time or money, be that paying for secretarial time, journal subscriptions, training, supervision, consultation, attendance at conferences and seminars, or engaging in teaching, mentoring, a professional development group or professional forum, or writing articles or books. It could be argued that if an independent social worker is claiming to have expert status then all of these activities come with the role so that the expert not only maintains their knowledge but is also participating in the development of knowledge in their particular field and for the next generation of practitioners. You also have to pay for accountancy services, a pension and professional indemnity insurance. Whatever else, an expert has to be businesslike and able to deliver on time and to the professional level expected – second rate is not acceptable. Being businesslike also means being able to pursue invoices with robust politeness before the cash-flow dries up. In short, quality costs. In order to provide a good-quality service that is sustainable, you have to factor in these costs to your fee structure and there needs to be a clearer understanding on the part of commissioners what the real cost of the service is. As a society, we also need to have some understanding of the cost in human terms, as well as financial, of not having well-versed experts available.

At the time of writing there is a serious challenge to independent social work experts in the form of Legal Services Commission (LSC) proposals that independent social worker expert witnesses should be paid £30 per hour outside London and £33 per hour in London. This contrasts with the range of fees proposed by the LSC for other professionals of £70 to £100 per hour. The government is seeking to dramatically reduce public spending and has been eyeing up the fees that experts charge for some time. BASW, the National Association of Guardians ad Litem and Reporting Officers (NAGALRO) and other organisations have lobbied the Ministry of Justice to rethink the proposed independent social work expert fee level and the Ministry of Justice has set up a reference group to gather first-hand facts about social work expert witnesses. £30 to £33 per hour does not recognise the cost of running an office, the years of experience, the skills, the knowledge and the competency required to function as an expert witness, and unlike some of our colleagues who are medical expert witnesses, we do not have a hospital base to cover all the administrative side of things. Ironically, while writing this book, someone drew our attention to an advertisement that made it clear that tattooists can expect to earn £70 per hour.

It is highly likely that independent social work expert witnesses will find that they cannot make a living with the proposed fee-scale and will withdraw from court work, potentially leaving some clients denied access to justice at a time when the political discourse is espousing the value of the family and stating that no frontline services will be cut. It is difficult to see how such a development can possibly be in anyone's best interests.

What about the future?

As politicians set about shaping the future, we as a profession must take every opportunity to demonstrate the intrinsic value of good-quality social work, in terms of both the impact it can have for individuals in their lives and for wider communities. We must also create opportunities to define the benefits that independent social work expert witnesses bring to the judicial process and to the lives of vulnerable people and to ensure that bodies such as the Ministry of Justice have a clear understanding of this. The risks of not doing this include a lack of access to well-informed justice and a society that is content to pay its expert social workers less than its electricians, mechanics and tattooists. While we have every respect for the skills and knowledge base of these diverse groups, surely the mechanics of human behaviour, the circuitry of social functioning and the self-image of vulnerable people call for a more complex level of understanding and a proportionate level of remuneration and recognition.

Chapter 8

Risk management

In the book entitled *Independent Social Work – A Risky Business?* (Tucker *et al.*, 2006) we concluded that while independent social work carried risks just like any other business and risk is a factor that always needs to be considered in relation to work with either individuals or organisations, independent social work provides an opportunity to effectively embrace risk and work with it constructively. For many independents, the risks were ones worth taking and were no greater than the risks of staying put in more traditional settings.

In the years since that book was published, it would be fair to say that independent social work *per se* has not become any less risky. It is also the case that the economic environment has brought increased levels of business risk. Therefore, the wise independent practitioner would be well advised to consider how they manage risks and how they reduce their exposure in recessionary times.

This chapter sets out a fairly standard model of risk assessment, one that many of us use quite subconsciously, and then goes on to consider it in the context of three main arenas – risk management in our business, risk management in our practice and risk management from a customer's perspective.

A basic model of risk management

First, know your own threshold for risk-taking. Try to quantify what level of risk is manageable or comfortable for you – this may be measured in financial terms, psychological terms or possibly both. It is important to be honest with yourself about your attitude to risk rather than being driven by a notion of what you think you ought to be able to cope with or what you imagine other people expect you to cope with. You are the one taking the risk, so it is your call.

Second, know the risks – identify and quantify them. The main questions to consider are

- What is the nature of the hazard?
- How likely is it to cause harm?
- What are the potential consequences?
- How serious are they?
- Who are they likely to affect?
- What are the potential positives if the risk is taken and succeeds?
- Do these potential benefits outweigh the potential negatives?

Having gained an understanding of the risks, identify ways to minimise them as far as possible and develop these into a risk management strategy. It is also important to recognise that some things are entirely beyond your control or your predictive abilities and just have to be dealt with when they arise, as many people found when harsh winter weather and volcanic ash clouds wreaked havoc on their diaries this year.

Last, review the risks regularly and make appropriate adjustments to your strategy.

Risk management in our business

Threshold for risk-taking

The types of questions you need to address include the following:

- What level of risk are you comfortable with?
- What can you (and your dependants) afford to lose if a contract goes wrong, if a customer doesn't pay up or if there simply isn't enough work around?
- If things do go wrong, do you have a fall-back position such as a contingency fund or someone who can assist you financially?

Knowing the risks

What are some of the factors that could have a negative impact on your business, particularly in these recessionary times?

- People paying their bills late or not paying at all, thus creating risk to cash-flow. This is one of the most basic reasons why small businesses get into difficulties, therefore it is important to understand how to maintain cash-flow and to develop a simple way of forecasting what money is due to arrive when.
- Getting behind with payments to Her Majesty's Revenue and Customs (HMRC).
- Unclear or unrealistic expectations, leading to a dispute. This might include an unclear or non-existent contract or unrealistic expectations about fees.
- Losing customers, possibly because they go out of business or because key contacts in organisations leave, thus reducing the likelihood of future work from that organisation.

- Bad publicity, perhaps because a piece of work has had a poor outcome or because someone has made negative or malicious comments about you or your practice.
- Being ill or having an accident, necessitating time off work.
- Other emergencies such as IT problems, communication systems failure, power failure, severe weather or industrial action causing travel disruption not to mention burglary or fire at your premises.

Formalise these in a written risk assessment, quantifying how great a risk they represent for you and what effects they might have. Then try to identify practical steps that you can take to minimise each risk. While this may seem an over-the-top approach, it is worth bearing in mind that our ability to be logical often evaporates in the face of a crisis so a well-thought out strategy can help overcome this if it is ever needed. The following paragraphs help illustrate some of the ways in which you might seek to minimise risks.

Minimising the risks

Cash-flow

- Set realistic fee levels for the work you are undertaking. Be aware of the overheads you have to cover along with the turnover that you need to achieve in order to be able to pay yourself a reasonable salary. In difficult financial times, there has to be some degree of flexibility in charges but not at any cost …
- Try to have several customers at any one time, thus spreading the risk. It is most unlikely that all your customers will fail to pay.
- Work for organisations with a proven track record of paying their bills or for organisations or individuals you have worked with before and who have proved reliable.

- Maintain good working relationships with your customers and communicate with them if difficulties do arise.
- Run a credit check or take references on new customers, particularly for large contracts.
- Negotiate terms of business that help your cash-flow. Standard practice in small businesses tends to be to expect payment within 30 days of invoicing the customer. However, many small businesses have adjusted their terms of business during these recessionary times to 14 days. Some have renegotiated terms of business so that payment is made on presentation of the invoice.
- Don't allow customers to run up large levels of debt – negotiate staged payments for substantial contracts.
- Be proactive in following up on late payments – don't assume that things will sort themselves out.
- Don't be afraid to be firm – it is your money. In extremis, if a customer continues to fail to pay and you have tried reasonable negotiation then a referral to the County Court can be a very effective and relatively inexpensive way to resolve the matter.

HMRC

- Be aware of all your tax liabilities and deadlines for payment and for submission of key documents such as self-assessments forms, company accounts, corporation tax and VAT returns and payments etc. Failure to meet deadlines will incur penalties.
- Plan ahead to ensure that you have funds available to meet your liabilities – consider having a separate bank account into which you make regular payments to ensure that you can meet your liabilities.
- Just in case you do find yourself in difficulties with HMRC, ensure that the deal that you negotiate with your accountant includes representation on such matters.

Unclear expectations

- Before starting any piece of work, irrespective of how large or small, ensure that there is a written agreement or contract that both you and your customer are happy with, which makes it clear who is going to do what, within what timeframe, at what cost and setting out terms of business. It is also wise to build in a mechanism for problem-solving or resolving disputes. This may all sound very obvious but we are aware of many instances where independent social workers and consultants have started a project in good faith without such an agreement being in place, then found it very difficult to set the parameters once they had begun. The rigour of developing such an agreement, and for larger projects developing a project plan, can often raise issues at an early stage. It can also work to your advantage as it often makes it clear just how complex the project is likely to be, thus it is easier to negotiate a realistic fee for the work.
- If negotiating such an agreement becomes fraught with difficulties then that too can be a helpful process in that it may be an indicator that this is a project that is best avoided.

Losing customers

- It is always good business practice to develop and maintain effective networks of contacts but this is particularly important in view of the ever-changing landscape in social work organisations at present. It is something of an art form to network well without being pushy and requires a willingness to contribute to the network as well as benefiting from it. Social workers' understanding of human relationships should serve them well in this regard.

Bad Publicity

- The obvious solution to bad publicity is to make every effort to ensure that there is never any cause for it. Don't be tempted to take on too much work or work that is outside your comfort zone or your expertise – be mindful of your Codes of Practice. Make sure that you keep up to date with developments in law, policy and practice to ensure that what you are providing is relevant and fit for purpose.
- If bad publicity does arise, whether malicious or well founded, deal with it. Get legal and professional advice, for example from a solicitor who specialises in defamation, or from BASW's Advice and Representation Service or from the legal helpline of the Federation of Small Businesses if you are a member of either.

Health problems

- Prevention is better than cure and any steps we can take to optimise our health and wellbeing will obviously be a good way of reducing this risk. However, it is almost inevitable that we will all need time off due to health difficulties or the effects of an accident at some point. It is therefore wise to identify what the likely implications would be for our business and to have some strategies for managing this. For example, if you work as a sole trader and you suddenly found that you could not work for six or eight weeks, is there another independent practitioner whom you could recommend to your customers who could carry out the work to a standard that you would be happy with? How would you meet your financial responsibilities during this time – do you have a contingency fund or do you have critical illness insurance in place? Are your working relationships with your customers sufficiently robust to allow you to negotiate a way forward in situations like this?

Other emergencies

Recession or no recession, emergencies such as the ones outlined above can arise at any time and the responses are as varied as the situations. However, the rule of thumb is that if you can think through and plan a response to keep things ticking over no matter what, then the chances of you maintaining continuity in your business are significantly higher. Many of these issues are covered in some detail in the previous book.

Risk management in our practice

Threshold for risk-taking

In our practice, the question of being clear about our comfort zone for risk-taking also applies and may well define the nature of the work that we undertake. In addition, we constantly need to review whether the types and levels of risk we are taking are consonant with our Common Law Duty of Care, our Codes of Practice and, for BASW members, our Code of Ethics. Last but certainly not least, we need to regularly review whether the risks we take are in our own best interests and whether we place ourselves at unacceptable levels of risk.

Knowing the risks – and minimising them

The risks identified in this section are not specific to recessionary times – they are constantly with us. The issue when times are tough is to resist the temptation to take unwise risks in order to get results or to save money or to benefit the business in some way.

What are some of the risks you might encounter in day-to-day practice? And how can you minimise them?

- Risk to personal safety when on visits. Try to identify situations that carry risk ahead of time and plan the location of the appointment to minimise risk. Let people know where you are and arrange to call them when the visit has ended. Agree a protocol for action if you have not checked in by a certain time. Consider having a tracker system fitted to your vehicle. If you are a BASW member, find out about Guardian24 – an electronic lone worker security system that is available to members. Above all, listen to your instincts about a situation.

- Risk of getting lost or being late – the real material of anxiety dreams for many an independent! The fact is that it can happen to any of us but the sensible thing to do is plan ahead, have clear directions and allow plenty of time when planning journeys. Don't rely solely on satellite navigation systems – they can be wrong, as the author can testify due to a recent experience of being directed onto the driveway of an unsuspecting citizen's property rather than into the car park of a training venue about a mile away.

- Risk of equipment failure at just the worst time, for example, arriving at a training venue to discover that your projector has blown a bulb (hopefully not on the same day that the satnav has misdirected you!). Even though it costs money, have equipment serviced regularly and keep spares of consumables in stock.

- Risk of giving advice which results in a bad outcome or making an assessment that is inaccurate. The best way to minimise this risk is to ensure that you keep your knowledge up to date and that you only accept work within your sphere of expertise. However, we have to acknowledge that this could happen to any of us no matter how conscientious we are, therefore the importance of carrying sufficient professional indemnity insurance such as the policy arranged by BASW Independents cannot be overemphasised.

- Risk of becoming overwhelmed by the nature of some of the work. Many independent social workers and consultants are contracted to work in extremely complex and emotionally draining situations because they have particular expertise that is not available within an organisation's own resources at the time in question. This carries the very real risk of physical and emotional exhaustion and it is imperative that practitioners pace themselves and ensure that they receive good-quality supervision or consultation. Any good social work business will cost this in as essential expenditure, not a luxury to be had in the good times.

- Risk of not being listened to or having your views marginalised. Independent social workers and consultants often have to impart difficult information to their commissioners, indeed it is often the reason why their expertise was sought in the first place. However, when it comes down to it, not all commissioning organisations are comfortable having their worst fears confirmed and may therefore try to minimise or marginalise the independent opinion. While there may be little that you can effectively do to prevent this, knowing what you know about human and thus organisational behaviour, you can minimise the effects it has through ensuring that the terms of engagement you draw up make it plain that a well-evidenced opinion still needs to be paid for even if it is unpalatable. You can also ensure that through good-quality supervision or consultation you clarify that the opinion was a reasonable one and that you have acted professionally. You can then also make a rational decision as to whether standing your ground is professionally the most appropriate thing to do or whether an exit strategy is the best option.

Risk management from a customer's point of view

Creating confidence for customers, whether they are private individuals or organisations, is one of the important first steps in developing a good working relationship. As the Personalisation Agenda in adult services rolls out, this will probably become a bigger issue in terms of working with individuals. In terms of organisations, many remain unsure how to contract with independent social workers or consultants and what the basic requirements ought to be.

Therefore, in terms of helping to set high standards of conduct, thus reducing the risk to customers, independent social workers and consultants can model good practice in the following ways:

- Inform people of your registration status with the GSCC or other regulatory body and show a copy of the registration document. Let people know that they can confirm this online and that there is a Code of Practice. Also make it clear that you are required to continue your learning and development as part of your registration and be prepared to show people evidence of this. (Be careful though that any evidence is not a breach of confidentiality or data protection legislation.)
- If you are a BASW member, tell people and let them know that you are therefore bound by BASW's Code of Ethics – give them a copy of this.
- Always consider whether any proposed work presents you with a conflict of interest and declare this if there is one.
- Inform your customers that they should carry out their own CRB checks on you at the level appropriate to the work you are going to carry out.
- Inform people that you carry professional indemnity insurance and Public Liability insurance and be prepared to show them the certificates.
- Inform people that you are registered as a Data Controller under the Data Protection Act and that you take every precaution in terms of managing their data in accordance with the law.
- Make sure that you have arrangements in place for supervision/ consultation and don't be afraid to tell people this.
- Make sure that there is a written agreement or contract in place to ensure that you and your customers have a clear understanding of your role and the terms of business.

Through modelling such good practice, conscientious practitioners can assist organisations and individuals develop their understanding of, and expectations of, independent social work practice and thus help them differentiate between good and bad practice. This can only be to the benefit of all concerned and a helpful strategy in terms of business development in difficult times.

You cannot eradicate all risk, even if you wanted to. What you can do, and must do if you are to develop your practice and your businesses in difficult times, is to be risk-aware and prepared to understand the risks and work with them in a responsible way.

Chapter 9

Transferable skills

Utilising theories of human behaviour and social systems, social work intervenes at the points where people interact with their environments.

This extract from BASW's Code of Ethics for Social Workers was written in 2001 to explain just what social work actually is. The very same art and science that is inherent in this extract can just as usefully be applied by independent social workers to their particular circumstances. Currently, those circumstances include both professional survival and meeting the challenges resulting from difficult economic times that will inevitably result from radical cuts proposed in public funding. In other words, the very nature of social work equips us to respond well to change and challenge.

Through their professional training, all social work students should have acquired the basic observational, assessment, analytical and reflective skills that form the bedrock of sound social work practice in any setting. Post-qualifying experience has the potential to further develop those individuals who go on to establish themselves as independent social workers at a later stage. It is within the workplace following social work qualification that the personal qualities so crucial for becoming a competent, respected independent social worker are developed. Those personal qualities include a capacity for hard work, for not scaring easily, for being confident, determined, flexible, committed to learn, self-motivated and able to apply skills in a range of settings. It is also within the early work environment that other vital components such as the promotion of human rights and the ensuring of social justice should have become a fundamental part of the individual's everyday, social work practice.

The wisdom gained during post-qualifying experience plus further learning and training opportunities means that over time the individual social worker's knowledge and skills set is likely to have become increasingly refined. It is this knowledge and skills set that the social worker will need to draw on when setting up in business as an independent social worker and subsequently developing that business in the challenging times ahead.

We outlined in our original book that independent social work is neither the easy option nor for the faint-hearted as it carries with it many professional and personal risks. However, the sheer number of individuals who have established themselves in private practice over the past decade evidences that this has become an increasingly attractive alternative to being either directly employed as a staff member or working as an agency worker. In recent years, social workers have operated within a climate where hostile, relentless and often misinformed media accounts of social work are commonplace. This situation, coupled with an intense public scrutiny of social work following a series of saddening, high-profile tragedies and scandals, has resulted in many employed social workers becoming disillusioned. Overwhelmed by a worrying workload, the burden of bureaucracy, paperwork, the heavy and complex caseloads they have carried plus a lack of support in some cases from managers who have themselves been under immense pressure through having insufficient staff to carry out complex statutory work, the cumulative effect has been a loss of morale and job satisfaction, with many social workers feeling themselves in minimal contact with the very people who attracted social workers to the job – people who use services. Unsurprisingly, in many organisations this situation has resulted in a revolving door of social workers as capable but increasingly anxious and dissatisfied staff have moved both into and then quickly out of jobs, sometimes too soon for their work to be properly evaluated and their practice held to account.

For those individuals who wish to take greater individual responsibility for the professional decisions they reach, who do not want to be bound by the same sort of restrictions that can limit work in many local authority settings, who want to feel more directly in control of their own caseload and especially those who wish to work more directly with people who use services, independent social work can seem a very attractive option.

It may be tempting to think that social care will not be quite so badly affected in the current round of cuts as other public services because it suffered so badly in past years in comparison to education or health. However, one only has to look at the freeze on social work recruitment in local government first in 1974 and then again in the 1980s to find precedents for this happening, so complacency has no place in current thinking. With an acute shortage of social workers, many local authorities have only been able to fulfil their legal obligations in recent years by contracting agency or independent social workers to plug these gaps. The probability is that in the near future many social care organisations will still have a labour and skills shortage and in this case may well need to rely on independent practitioners in order to meet their statutory commitments. In short, in dire circumstances there are always winners and losers and during the current recession this may well mean that there are opportunities for independent social workers.

Most recently, commissioners have looked to contract independent practitioners to plug gaps that their own, in-house services have been unable to provide. Sometimes this has been because of a shortage of staff, sometimes because a wholly independent perspective has been required, sometimes because the situation has become too hot for the organisation to want to handle. In these circumstances, an independent who has a good skills and knowledge base, a high reputation and a proven expertise in managing a business which brings with it an established infrastructure, can be very attractive. This is because they will have in place their own telephone, email and usual office facilities, their own transport, responsibility for their own training, learning and development and a capacity to manage their own timetable in order to give value for money at a time of reduced budgets and high pressure on managers' time.

Even in recessionary times, there is the potential for organisations and individuals still wanting to buy in a safe pair of hands for specific pieces of work. These will be in cases where the independent social worker can provide value for money and provide work of a high standard conducted in an ethical manner and delivered on time without the commissioner manager having to take further responsibility for it until the conclusion. Despite the difficult times expected, there are potential opportunities for independent practitioners – the real skill lies in knowing just how to exploit them. Some practical tips follow to help you in this process.

Do's and don'ts

Do consider cost effectiveness. It is in the interests of both parties in recessionary times – the commissioner and the commissioned – to consider the limited amount of money available for the contract. Both parties will benefit if the work is completed in as cost-effective a manner as possible and if the expenditure is transparent. If there is obvious value for money then the commissioner may well commission further pieces of work. Take every opportunity to demonstrate how your input represents best value.

Do ensure when diversifying or taking on a different area of work that it is not substantially outside your comfort zone and expertise. If it is a piece of work that poses too much of a risk, this has the potential for being both professionally irresponsible as well as contravening BASW's Code of Ethics.

Do be as flexible as possible. As with any self-employment, making yourself available when the work is there is essential. Sometimes this may be inconvenient, involving travel some distance away from an office base for example, but being willing to take on such work may help the commissioner and result in the commissioner feeling favourably disposed towards the independent who has assist d.

Do develop a broad portfolio of work and customers. Too much specialisation can restrict the amount or types of work that you are approached to undertake. There is a cautionary tale concerning an independent social worker who set up as a specialist in life story work after becoming frustrated by the paperwork when an employed social worker in a child care permanency team. Her former colleagues increasingly referred children from the team to her – to the point where she was working full-time but only on commissions for her former employers. A change of manager soon put paid to this arrangement for although the independent practitioner was carrying out high-quality work, this was expensive. When the new manager was required to make savings in her budget she arranged for a small group of her staff to attend life story training and, in turn, to disseminate that learning to the remainder of their colleagues. As a direct result, the independent social worker quickly lost her sole source of income.

Do work hard at maintaining an active involvement with people who are likely to commission services. Utilise opportunities to network that present themselves, such as when attending meetings in different agencies. Making time to be present at leaving parties for people who have previously commissioned a service can not only be a way of thanking them for their commissions and wishing them well but can also provide an opportunity to meet the new person in that role. Of course, not everyone who leaves does so due to retirement: many go on to other positions where they might welcome the input from a trusted independent practitioner.

Do ensure that you maintain an involvement with other social workers in a similar area of work. Such involvement can be invaluable and can come about through maintaining a friendship group with former colleagues, through involvement with BASW's Independents or via peer supervision.

Do use times when the work dips in as productive a way as possible. It is an appealing option to use a slack period after a particularly busy time in order to recharge one's batteries but it may be more important in recessionary times to think both long term as well as about the immediate future. For example, tempting though it may be to take an afternoon off, it may be more productive to use this time for reading, for research, for keeping up to date or for acquiring/developing a further skill, which could prove attractive to future commissioners.

Do consider that the same analytical skills that are part and parcel of everyday practice can usefully be transferred. Assess just what it is that you need to do to develop a more rounded professional portfolio or to comply with and demonstrate that you have engaged in post-registration training and learning (PRTL). Plan how to extend a knowledge base, giving careful consideration to whether this can be acquired through self-directed research or reading rather than paying out for a training course.

Do explore if there are alternative, less expensive ways to acquire the further knowledge and requirements for re-registration as a social worker. For example, instead of paying to attend costly day conferences, which although tax deductible as a legitimate work expense also mean that there will be no earnings that day, consider instead whether it would be appropriate to attend a Community Care Live event or the occasional BASW meeting. Several of these attract attendance records, which could meet your PRTL requirements.

Do think outside the box about training. For example, an independent social worker who is also a school governor has found that the Governing Body Support Unit has excellent training courses relating to looked-after vulnerable children, children with special educational needs, inclusion and exclusion, the impact of domestic violence and similar courses, with the training equally relevant for her work as an independent practitioner as for her voluntary work. A bonus of such training is that no fee is attached to it and it takes place in the evenings. This has meant it has been extremely cost-effective.

Do remember that the most complex cases are still likely to require an independent opinion. Be aware, though, when taking on such work that it could be the proverbial hot potato so it is vital to feel able to refuse the work if it is too controversial.

Do remember, too, that it is not only a global financial recession that can bring about a change in your circumstances. Personal events can have a similar effect. For example, illness affecting you or a member of your family, separation, divorce, bereavement and becoming a carer are all issues that can bring about a different type of recession. This can change your personal outlook, may require you to relocate, change your hours of work or make other adjustments to your lifestyle.

Don't be a 'one-trick pony'. You may prefer a particular type of work but if noone wishes to buy in this expertise then you would be better researching then extending a skill set in order to offer a service that is required.

Don't put 'all your eggs in one basket'. See the example regarding the life story work that was given earlier as an example of the folly of only doing work for one agency.

Don't dismiss the importance of using all opportunities that present themselves as times for raising your profile/networking. Sometimes these will come at inconvenient times and may seem costly in terms of time spent but the importance of developing and continuing relationships with people who may commission services cannot be overstated.

Don't rule out a return to a previous area of work/specialism if work presents in that arena. For example, a social work consultant who has worked in adult services for more than ten years was approached about assisting with a contract in children's services. To begin with she considered turning it down because of the time since she practised in that area of work – until she reminded herself that her first 20 years' practice in child protection would ably equip her for a return to such a role.

Don't take on work too far outside your comfort zone or expertise. Understandably and appropriately, many people like the challenge of taking on new areas of work that both stretch and challenge existing knowledge and skills. Remembering that it is important to be extended, it is also vital and professionally responsible not to extend too far. Our Codes of Conduct reinforce that you should offer suitable referral onwards when service users' needs fall outside the level of your own competence.

Don't underestimate the importance of social work consultation. In cash-strapped times, it may be more cost-effective to form a peer supervision group with other, like-minded individuals instead of buying in individual social work consultation. However, experience teaches that peer group supervision is most successful when groups take place locally, where individuals share a common area of interest or specialism and where priority is given to attending such meetings.

Don't forget to look after yourself. In difficult times, looking after your health and taking appropriate breaks can help to manage the stress of the work. It is also important to manage the volume of work you take on and to manage your diary effectively.

Don't discount a mixed economy of work. If work is in short supply, for example, consider taking on part-time work either as an employed or as an agency worker alongside commissions as an independent social worker, provided that this work is openly declared and does not pose any conflict of interest. Remember, too, that it is ethically incorrect to use opportunities as a paid employee to solicit for independent work.

Last, don't forget that an independent social worker is only ever as good as the last piece of work. You may have had many years of working very ably but if a court assessment, for example, is delivered late or is of poor quality it is likely to be this that is remembered and not all the previous, high-quality pieces of work. A reputation for not delivering on time could result in you being overlooked in another case – which could be a major concern in recessionary times.

In conclusion

As stated earlier, there is no room for complacency in our thinking. There is already a worrying shortage of social workers and a potential recruitment freeze, high workloads, a lack of confidence and morale and negative perceptions of social work. However, there is room for creativity and optimism that the independent role can become even more pivotal. It can be argued that delivering complex pieces of work on time and to a very high standard will be even more desirable as local authorities look not only to cut costs but also to improve performance, all the while under considerable public scrutiny. The well-positioned independent – someone with experience, transferable skills and a reputation for delivering high-quality assessments and analysis – is likely to be essential to organisations achieving this in the future despite the recessionary times ahead.

Some final thoughts

So, having read these chapters and considered the views expressed in them, when the going gets tough, *are* you tough enough? What does it take to be tough enough in these austere and remarkably fluid times? Is being tough the same as being aggressive? We argue not.

The toughness to survive as an independent social worker or consultant is much more akin to resilience – aggression has no part to play, although assertiveness clearly does. This type of toughness derives much more from having an intelligent understanding of the role of independent social work and the immense potential of the role, a clear vision of the marketplace and your position within it, a realistic understanding of your strengths and weaknesses and a willingness to negotiate sensibly but firmly to ensure best value for customers without selling yourself short.

It also calls for a well-founded and well-grounded belief in your abilities combined with an ability to market those appropriately and to constantly ensure that your knowledge and skills are up to date. It calls for a good understanding of how to manage business and professional risk and to manage money carefully. It requires flexibility and a readiness to diversify – but only within responsible limits. Above all, it calls for a strong sense of commitment to your chosen profession, the ethical underpinning of the profession and to the people it serves.

There can be no doubt that we are in for interesting times ahead as recessionary pressures bite and the political agenda unfolds. We can see it as a time either of threat or of opportunity. If it feels like a time of threat then independent social work or consultancy may not be the right option for you. However, if you are prepared to embrace the opportunity and are confident that you have what it takes, then it may be that you can play a part in reshaping the social work landscape at this critical time.

It is your call...

References

Darwin, C. (1859) *The Origin of Species by Means of Natural Selection*, London, John Murray.

DH (Department of Health) (2001) *Carers and People with Responsibility for Disabled Children: Practice Guidance* London, DH.

DH (2008) *Carers at the Heart of 21st Century Families and Communities* London, DH.

Favez, J. C. (1999) *The Red Cross and the Holocaust* (translated by John Fletcher) Cambridge, Cambridge University Press.

Tucker, G., Sambidge, A. and Ogilvy, H. (eds) (2006) *Independent Social Work – A Risky Business?* Birmingham, BASW/Venture Press.